When I was young and couldn't properly see,
I was poked and prodded for being me.

This left an old scar which was embedded inside,
And often at times I would love to just hide!

But now is the time, for in truth I am ready,
To get back on my feet, yes, nice and steady.

I stand tall as the beauty that I eternally am,
Across the great channel of water I swam.

To reach the side of sun and grace,
Where I can truly reveal my face!

Lee-Anne Peters

Category: New Age Publications; Self Help; Biography

Temple of Balance the book

Author: Lee-Anne Peters

Tasmania, Australia

ABN: 68 727 281 953

http://thebook.templeofbalance.com

Email: mail@templeofbalance.com

First printed / published by Temple of Balance Publishing in April 2011.

Edited by Lee-Anne and Cory Peters

Illustrated and Designed by Lee-Anne Peters

Printed and bound in China.

Peters, Lee-Anne 1976 -

ISBN: [978-0-9870708-0-7]

Temple of Balance

the book

Lee-Anne Peters

Are You Ready to Be Inspired?

Temple of Balance Publishing
Inspiring ~ Creating ~ Empowering

Books by Lee-Anne Peters

From Lack to Abundance: *Keys to Manifesting Your Success!*

Aligning with the Speed of Light: *A Guide to Ascension!*

Temple of Balance the book: *Are you ready to be Inspired?*

eBooks by Lee-Anne Peters

Eternal Love: *A True Story About Twin Flames!*

Healing Energy Cards companion

Card Decks by Lee-Anne Peters

Healing Energy Cards: *Tools to help you Self Heal!*

Temple of Balance Oracle Cards: *Guidance from our friends in spirit!*

CD's by Lee-Anne Peters

Grounding Meditation Journeys CD

Coming soon

Meditation: Simple & Effective

Speed of Light Oracle

Ascension Mastery Series Part II – I Am Goddess

Dedication

For my amazingly supportive, husband Cory, your love and gentleness are always cherished more than words can say.

For Sean; my energetic and artistic young man.

For Madison; my bubbly and creative young woman.

I love the three of you very much.

Thank you to Jane Sleeman for gracing Cory and I with your positivity, love and enthusiasm for life. You were an inspiration and it was our honour to know you. Flying Free Beautiful Angel!

To everyone who has been a part of Temple of Balance over the years. Thank you.

I am grateful to every experience I have had in my life, they have all led me up to now.

Contents

Exercises

I AM Goddess, I dance & shine.

I AM full of life - there is no need to hide.

I step out from my hiding place, and up to the door.

I let go of the past, I commit to it all.

I step through it now, with eagerness and excitement.

I AM woman, I AM Goddess, I AM ME!

Lee-Anne Peters

Preface

Welcome to my first book; **Temple of Balance the book!** Full of inspiring information about all things I am passionate about, and loads of practical exercises to help you move forward in your life. This book is sure to inspire you to pull out your own book ideas, to step out of fear and choose love, to know that you do in fact have the power within you to heal yourself, and to discover the numerous benefits there are when you trust your inner guidance or intuition!

Temple of Balance is a business I founded in February 2005, and has grown because of the high integrity, love and passion that has been invested into it since its conception. Consider for a moment about the words Temple of Balance and what they may personally represent for you.

Here are my ideas; Your Temple is represented by your body – your Temple that houses *your* spirit. And the word Balance represents the Balance, harmony, alignment and evenly flowing energy within your Temple – your body! So Temple of Balance inspires you to find Balance within, and to love and honour your body, your Temple that contains your spirit!

When your Temple is Balanced and harmonised within, this then reflects out into all areas of your life. Transforming your world into one, that is in alignment with your new sense of inner Balance and peace.

Since founding Temple of Balance I have worked full time being of service to others and our planet. When I say 'being of service' I am not meaning that I am a servant or a slave to anyone or anything. It means to me that I give and dedicate a lot of my day helping others in any way I can. When I am being of service I also include myself in this, because to me it is extremely important to maintain that balance in all areas, which in turn allows me to be able to help others more. I am always looking for different ways to help, and also I understand that not everyone resonates with everything, so I offer many different approaches and I trust that people who are ready will find something useful for their personal needs and their highest good.

Through the creation of online communities, online and local meditations, various services, workshops, healing art, e-newsletters and other things I feel that more people are finding the help they need via whichever method worked best for them.

This book, **Temple of Balance the book** is an extension of this *helpline* and one that I feel will reach and assist people who I may not have met online. I envision this book being in the hands of a wide variety of people from all across the world. And I trust it brings you great joy, inspiration and the energy that you require in the moments it is in your hand!

This is time for you. Time for you to; connect with your body, your breathing and your essence. As you read I trust that you are also inspired to follow your dreams, even if they are only small steps taken every day (yes, this does count). The more you step into your power, the more empowered you become to truly live and love. Please don't be afraid to be you, to love who you are and to enjoy your life. Your life is about you!

I feel that everyone has the power to heal themselves; it's just that many people don't have the tools they need to do it. **Temple of Balance the book** may assist you in that area.

Temple of Balance the book is an exciting first book for me; it talks about the founding of my online self-help business; Temple of Balance and my journey of self healing and spiritual awakening. Some of this journey began earlier in my life (before the founding of Temple of Balance) and sometimes even right back into the long distant past, in a whole other time and space. As I wrote this book I was guided by my spiritual teachers to include practical exercises to help you with your self healing, letting go and various other things. This inspiring book also is the first time I have ever shared one of my Intuitive Energy Healing sessions in full. You can read all about it in chapter 8, and also receive some healing for yourself.

This book contains a lot of healing energy, and as you read you may feel energy moving in your body, this is very normal and is a signal from your body that you are letting go, healing and experiencing changes within. I ask that you breathe through any emotions, mental or physical effects that may surface for you. They come to your attention so you can move out of fear and pain, and move deeper into your freedom and love. So you can heal!

I suggest to my clients and my event participants who visit me in person, to help you flow smoothly with this experience; please allow yourself to feel and flow. If any old energy surfaces for you as you read, I recommend that you *drink lots of water*, to help flush the old energy from your body; *listen to your body*, if it wants to rest, eat a different type of food and so on, then please honour this. Your body is a very sensitive instrument; it will help you know what you *need* to restore balance. *Be kind and gentle with yourself;* avoid all harsh words towards yourself. Pay attention to what thoughts you think and words you say and if they are not nourishing, then please stop that thought or word and reprogram it with a positive thought. You can get back in control of your life!

My passions are to help others love and accept who they are and to follow their dreams. Contained within the cover of this book is how I have done this in my life, as I feel we teach others best by sharing our story. Within us all is our own life story. It's what we choose to create with our life that I am very passionate about.

For me, I consciously began my self-healing journey when I was 24. I say *consciously* because for approximately a decade before then, I had been exploring the 'new age' world with much excitement. I recall staying with my mother when I was about fourteen (my parents separated when I was very young) and I was shown a set of 'Mythic tarot cards' that someone gave her - my mother never used them. I began to read and study them and I don't think they left my side that whole weekend. It was to my delight that my mother offered them to me. I studied the cards, played with them and learnt all the stories behind each one. A year or so later when I went to college (years 11 & 12 in my country) was when I began to do a lot of readings for others. I remember having students lining up for readings during school breaks in the cafeteria. It was great fun and just the beginning for me.

As I reflect back I notice that at the time I had no awareness or knowledge of the spirit world. I was lucky enough to have no substantial deaths in my family until

I was 24. However I know that this phase was all preparation for what would occur for me later in life.

I trust what you connect with within this book inspires you to be more of who you are, while empowering you to know that you really can do anything and create your life the way you want it to be! You will find many ways in this book to help you relax, experience joy, to feel and heal.

Thank you for coming with me on this journey. It has been an amazing one for me. A journey of immense joy and happiness, mixed with trial and error. It is my honour to expand what I have learnt during my own self healing journey and flow it into your heart. I receive so much joy when I help others. In the coming pages you will see and experience Temple of Balance's journey from my perspective.

I feel completely honoured that **Temple of Balance the book** is here, in your hands!

In wholeness and harmony,

Lee-Anne Peters

March 2011

Tasmania, Australia

Section 1 - The Beginning

Chapter 1 - Before the Beginning

I stood high on the weathered cliff, my wavy, long, sandy blonde hair cascading down my long slender back. The windswept it softly as I gazed out to the vast sea before me. I reflected on the great city where I lived. You may remember this city; it is known as Atlantis.

The time is 11,000 Earth years ago, one of my first Earthly incarnations. I have clear visions of being *'dropped off'* to Earth from the stars. I was sent here with my Twin Flame to accomplish a very important mission. This mission has been long and tiring; yet very rewarding. I have seen it all. This lifetime is the final of our mission, yet we still have much to do and create. I know I have certain guidelines and 'boxes' to mark off when I complete tasks in this lifetime, however I have decided that I am not *only* going to complete those tasks assigned to me, but I am striving to accomplish more! I will not just settle for those 'marked boxes' that make my mission, I am going to make this life count and this life the very best!

For this lifetime it has been like a *remembering* for me. I remembered quickly and early. Some people take a long time to learn these things, but not me. Some say it's because I am very grounded and Down-to-Earth. However I feel it is because it is time for me to shine in the beauty and love that I am and to help others shine too by my living example. I have had hundreds of lifetimes of experience, and this lifetime is all about *remembering.*

It was warm in Atlantis, and this climate suited me perfectly. I wore long flowing gowns, lined with silver and golden trims and I would often place flowers in my hair.

As I gaze up to the land above me, there stood a great Temple. This is my creative space; in this Temple is where I help others.

I wander over the soft green grass to the Temple entrance. The air is very fresh and light. There is a *'lightness'* to everything. Like a crystalline glow. The entrance is very grand, marked with stone pillars and a bright blue and red speckled floor. I enter the main foyer where there's a beautiful and peaceful atmosphere, lots of fresh air, paintings line the walls and murals on the ceiling. Beyond the main foyer is a sacred room, this is where I created. This was my healing space. I created my healing back then in a very unique and sacred way. Times were different, there was no disease like now, no stress, no germs, there was much more harmony within the body, mind and emotions for people in general. There were no 'doctors' as we know them in 'modern' times, but there were sacred priests, not religious, but magical! They could instantly heal wounds and physical damage. For me, I had a very different role; I was working a lot with *specially selected* children. Helping them open up to their unique healing gift and be able to use it in a safe and flowing way. Healing to me is simply change that contributes to our growth on all levels. The healing was harmonious and worked a lot with energy. Healers were accepted among society in early Atlantean times. I worked a lot with people to help them adjust to the *denseness* of Earth's energy. Although the Earth is much denser now, in Atlantis it was denser than most of the Atlantean's 'home in the stars.'

During this lifetime as a healing priestess, I worked a lot with crystals and sacred stones. I was a very compassionate, generous and peaceful soul. I loved my time in Atlantis, and this may be where I first met you!

You see in this lifetime now; just prior to when Temple of Balance was founded, I was told by spirit that I would be in my Temple again. This bought me so much joy to know this. At the time I assumed it was a physical Temple, however it wouldn't be long and I would find out that wasn't the plan at all. Well not yet anyway.

I was also told that many of the people I worked with in Atlantis (clients and friends) would reconnect with me in this lifetime. And I have been privileged to meet many of these souls again since Temple of Balance was created.

The signs had been getting stronger and stronger and on the 25th of February 2005 at the age of 29 my life changed. Temple of Balance was created. It was created in a most amazing way. For several months I knew I was going to be in my temple again, but how and when? I did not know, and I certainly didn't expect it to be like this...

Chapter 2 – The Healing Temple Reborn

I remember this day as my youngest sister, Erica's birthday. It was around lunch time when I needed to arrange the internet for my family's new house. After travelling with them in the caravan up the East coast of Australia for two years and having an awesome time, it was time to settle my young children into school. So I hadn't really had the internet before this time.

I called our main internet provider and proceeded to start connecting my computer to the internet. When the representative asked me over the phone; what I would like my email address to be, I went blank! Had I have known he was going to ask me this I would have given it some thought, but no time to think. He suggested my name, but hey, everyone did that back then. So I mentioned to him that I wanted something more creative, something different than just my name. The representative asked me what my passions were. I mentioned healing and spiritual things. We threw back some ideas and he said, what about *'Temple of Ascension.'* Then it hit me, I knew it had to be *'Temple of Balance.'* At that time I had been learning a lot about balance on many levels. This felt so right. So it was then and there, in that moment, that Temple of Balance was born!

I was incredibly excited and felt a brewing passion rise within me. I could sense that this was the beginning of something amazing. A sensational journey was presenting itself perfectly.

At long last I was in my Temple again.

Chapter 3 – eBay

Upon returning to my home state of Tasmania, Australia after travelling, I was looking for ways to earn an income from home. I was a hairdresser by trade, but was not interested in getting back into it again. My youngest child was just starting her first year at school part time, and I really wanted to be there before and after school for my children at their young age. I wanted to enjoy as much time with my children as possible before they grow up and leave the nest.

Many people didn't understand what I wanted to do. They saw that I was a trained hairdresser and they wanted me to keep cutting people's hair whilst I wished I was elsewhere. As you may know I am not easily influenced by others, and I certainly am not a sheep. I like being unique. So I stuck to my guns and explored doing something online to bring a bit of an income. I followed my intuition.

My first attraction to eBay was at my sister Louise's house when I noticed that people were selling art and doing clairvoyant readings there. The art side wasn't attracting me at the time, but I explored eBay and added a few clairvoyant reading listings.

I had never done a distant reading before, so I was a little apprehensive. Especially when someone sent me a message; asking me to 'tell them something that was happening in their life, so they knew I was genuine and they would purchase a reading from me.'

I sat at my computer thinking - what on Earth was I doing! My spirit guide came forward to help me. He told me to 'calm down, ask the question to the cards and lay them out in front of me.' With no-one in front of me to talk to or ask questions to, I had to trust that what I was seeing and typing to my client was accurate and what they needed. As a result the man was happy and purchased a reading. That was my first one via distance, which would turn out to be the first of many.

I met some wonderful people on eBay and many of them I still connect with now. I feel very fortunate to have had an eBay experience!

From here on Temple of Balance continued to expand, and very quickly at that!

Chapter 4 – Expansion

I was so excited to be doing what I loved for people in the comfort of my own home, and it was working. I was guiding people with things that even surprised me. Messages from deceased loved ones, dates and information about the future, which I would later have verified. I began to expand my repertoire to include healings, spirit guide messages, karmic healing, past life readings and spiritual drawings. This is where my passion became more aroused. Within six months I was so busy that I was booked out for 6 – 8 weeks in advance. I was working full time during school hours and couldn't believe how well everything flowed and expanded. The sad thing was that I noticed so many people needed help.

I began offering my distant services overseas, and at one stage had more clients in America than my home country of Australia. It was totally incredible.

In my home life, I continued to have very little to no support from my family, and often I felt that my clients knew me better than they did. Through it all my spiritual guides were amazing. One in particular I had been working with for many years would help me and acknowledge my efforts. This was very comforting for me.

Now I am in a whole new space. After making huge changes in my personal life, I am now lucky enough to have a beautiful husband and children. My husband is very supportive and in fact works at Temple of Balance with me. Together, as a male & female we form *'a'* *Temple of Balance,* and this we intend to inspire in others who are ready and willing.

eBay listings began to get quite expensive as their fees continued to rise and with a nice client base now, I created a website.

My website gave me the freedom to create. I created it and adapted it to suit my client's needs. I developed many different services and ways to help people as much as I could.

In the next chapters I will be sharing my experience and what I learnt from these services that I did both on myself and others. Within these pages you will find empowering exercises and tools to help you in your life now.

Section 2 - Healing

Chapter 5 – Distant Healing Miracles

Many people who practised clairvoyance, medium-ship or healing that I spoke to really struggled to understand how distant healing (online) was possible, let alone successful. Few were eager to hear my stories, so I just let it be.

With such successful results I was curious as to how this all worked. I didn't have a client in front of me; in fact often I only worked with a name and birth date.

I learnt that when we, as healers, work with people via distance we are working beyond the dimension of time and space. We are immediately connecting in with the 5th dimension of Love. This was a profound realisation for me, and made so much sense. So in other words, because my client was not with me physically and was often on the other side of the world, even in my past according to time zones, this high vibrational energy would reach them immediately. In fact many times the healing began the moment the session was committed to.

When a distant healing session is organised with a client, I ask them for their name and anything else they would like to share. Some people share a lot and others nothing, I trust that they are following their intuition and do what is needed. Then I schedule their session. It doesn't matter what time or day it is, or what they are doing, the energy will reach them in that moment.

It's all about intention. As we hold our intentions to do things, talk to people, go here or there, our energy moves ahead in time and space, and begins to help create that future moment. Intentions are very, very powerful.

Chapter 6 – Trust and Intuition

I have learnt so much about trust. This has been an amazing experience in the fact that I have been taught to let my mind / ego go and trust in the flow of the moment.

How can I do this? How can I just switch off my mind and not worry if what I am saying is right, or whether they will accept what is being said or not? Well, I can't worry about any of these things. When I worry about it, I actually attract doubt and errors to me, because like attracts like. If I am confident and fully trusting then that is what I attract. I attract the truth. I trust I am a clear channel of truth.

Many years ago during a shamanic drumming meditation, our group focus was on the third eye chakra. A chakra is an energy centre that draws in life force and energy to help our mind, spirit, body and emotions flow in a harmonious manner. During this meditation journey I was shown a clear vision about what trust is. This helped me a lot. I find that at times many of us are too hard on ourselves if we had a feeling to do something or go somewhere or even just say something, we shrug it off and then later on we reflect back and punish ourselves for not following what we felt, and 'why do I always do that?' – we often ask ourselves.

The important thing with trust is to understand that it is a process and as long as you are learning during this process then you **are** in fact trusting.

This meditation vision showed me an image of a wall under construction. Each brick on this wall represented trust. I was shown by spirit that each time we do trust our body or trust our intuition then we place another block on our *'wall of trust.'* However the interesting part is that every time we don't follow through with these intuitions, but later we see that we *could* have and we make the commitment to ourselves that 'next time; I will follow through with these feelings' then we also place another brick contribution on our trust wall.

The point is that as long as we are not too hard on ourselves and we are self reflective, noticing what we could have done differently and that we will take note for the next time while staying true to ourselves, we are in fact, learning and establishing our trust.

There are different forms of trust; self trust and trusting in the flow of life.

I recall my first observation about trusting flow when I was hairdressing. I would see clients with all sorts of different hair types, growth patterns, some with curls, and others with limp / fine hair. Most clients who sat in the chair wanted their hair different to how it naturally was, and yes this could be done to a degree, however you could not change what the hair growth wanted to do. Hair on the head grows in a spiral from the crown and when hair is cut in its natural flow you get no resistance. Which means 'less areas' that 'stick up' or 'sit funny.' After this realisation I began to cut and style hair to suit the natural flow. And this natural flow always manifested into something beautiful.

When we trust / follow the natural flow then things work out. It doesn't mean that we sit back and let the world happen around us. If you want to change your experience and you don't want to continue living the same life day in and day out, then it is up to you to make changes. In fact when we look to nature and the cycles of day and night, and the seasons too, we notice that it is natural for things to change and flow with the change. We don't see animals complaining about how cold or hot it is today. The more we try and force things to stay the way they used to be, the more energy we waste trying to swim upstream, it eventually creates a burden on the body, mind and emotions and it can affect every area of our life.

Commit to change, trust the flow and listen to your beautiful body. Your body is a sensitive instrument and is a very powerful tool that will help you in every area of your life. Spend some time nourishing and honouring your body, it is the temple that houses your spirit. **Your,** Temple of Balance.

When it comes to my work and trusting the flow it is incredibly essential that I trust my body, my client's energy and my spiritual guides, one hundred percent. I must be confident and trusting to allow whatever energy the client needs for their highest good to flow through in that moment. Not what they think they need or what I think they need, but what they truly need for their personal growth, highest good and evolvement. I have learnt that when I trust in this flow then miracles happen. Trusting this flow allows my spiritual guides to tap into my experience, my knowledge and do what is necessary for my client at the time. Because I am fully open in the moment and with the flow, often new healing techniques come through that I have never done or heard of before. This shows me that there is awesome power at work behind the scenes, and when we open up to the source miracles can happen.

I must point out here that whilst I become sensitive to my client during a healing session, I do this so I can feel what my client feels in order to heal, clear and release with them. I do not take on other people's issues or pain. The reason I don't is because I don't allow myself to. I care for every client I work with, however I do not place them above myself. We must always consider our own health and well being so we can be of the highest service for others, if that is what we are drawn to do.

As I connect with my client for distant healing I tune into their energy and feel what is happening using my own body as a guide. If I feel pressure around my head or get a head ache, usually it is because my client has been thinking or worrying a lot and it is creating a strong energy pressure on the head. If my client has an issue with communicating or suppression of their truth, then I may feel a block or change in energy around my throat.

I must be fully in tune with my body to do this. When I build a strong connection with my body, I not only recognise what is not my energy, but I can also be a clearer channel of healing energy for my client.

Many people are very sensitive to energy and can walk in a room and feel tension or unease in the air. If at any time you are concerned that you have 'picked up' foreign energy, then try this simple exercise if it feels right to you.

Exercise (i): Clearing foreign energy from your system

Place your feet flat on the floor, breathe deeply and gently, then say three times with confidence and knowing, that **'if this is not my pain, then please leave immediately.'**

The pain **will** leave straight away if it is not your energy. If it remains, then there is something in it that you are tied to. So do some self reflecting and healing for as long as you feel the desire, and it will be sure to release.

The more I gained knowledge, skills, tools and experience from my journey reading and learning, the more help I could be to others. I began exploring sound healing, healing through colour and art, energy work and clearing, spiritual surgery, DNA activation, awakenings, grounding, balancing and the list goes on.

It is my opinion you do not 'need' to spend thousands of dollars on fancy courses and initiations. The most valuable skills you can acquire are through your own life experience. Please don't give your power away to others to solve your life, to fix your problems, to teach you things etc. stand tall in your power and inner strength and take the action that you feel is right for you. Don't do these things out of a 'need.' Do them out of a passion that brews within you. An inner urge from your guides, that you trust and follow through with. Don't underestimate your own personal power!

Chapter 7 – Spiritual Helpers

I began to really consciously work with my spirit guides very early on in my spiritual awakening. Funny for me is that this connection would begin after a spirit guide drawing from a beautiful spiritual artist visiting my town. I felt so excited to have my spirit guide from Atlantis drawn and I began to really connect with the drawing and my guide.

Around six months after that I had a dream that I painted an Indian. The dream was so vivid; I still remember it so clearly. The very next morning I got out my pastels and began to draw what I dreamt. What evolved was an amazing Indian with feathers in his hair. I began talking to him a lot, and learnt that his name is 'Red Eagle' and that he was a shaman or medicine man.

Red Eagle taught me so much. He divinely led me to a local shamanic meditation drumming group where I remained for about 5 years. He helped me learn about balance and being grounded. Also about energy work, healing and connecting with nature and power animals. Red Eagle told me that he is my main 'master' spirit guide and that he had been with me since my conception in this life. Red Eagle taught me how important it is to not be 'ruled' by spirit guide's messages and guidance, and how important it is to walk side by side with spirit guides, and not feel that they always lead the way!

Spiritual guides are learning, just as we are. Their advantage is that they perceive what is happening to us from a spirit perspective. They are not in the middle of the drama. This can be very helpful when we feel 'stuck' in a present situation. We can ask for their help and pay attention for guidance.

Everyone has spirit guides, this I know as a fact, I have seen it. Actually, many of us have many spiritual guides. For those of you who are interested in working with yours, you will have quite a few. Even those people who think there is no truth in this 'stuff' will have a couple. The more we call on our guides and work with them, the stronger relationship we build with them. When we do this, we attract more and more spiritual beings into our energy space to work with.

I work with mine a lot, and have over one hundred who just help me with healing work. You see, everything we do in our life attracts help from spirit. Each 'role' we play in our daily life brings a different spirit guide to help us.

When my son was about six years old, he was having a play in the bath tub one evening when he called out to me with a sense of alarm in his voice. He told me that he felt someone touch his back. I stood still, took a deep breath and felt a little boy in spirit playing with him in the bath. I mentioned this to him; he smiled cautiously and felt the same. He then continued to play and started talking to the boy who was in spirit.

Whether it is food shopping, exercise, work, study, visiting others, meditating, relaxing in bed or spending time with friends, we have different guides who join us for those different roles we play. If you pay attention to your body and energy, you may even notice it slightly change as you move from one role to the next.

To utilise your spiritual guides' help, you must start to call them into your life. You don't need to know their name. If you do, great, call on them via this title. If you don't know a name yet, either refer to them as 'my guides' or imagine a name that seems fitting. Honestly, your guides don't mind what you call them, they just love working with you.

Since 2005, when I founded Temple of Balance, I have been doing a lot of spirit guide channelling and drawing for clients all around the world. So I have a lot of experience personally with spiritual guides.

Usually when you are first building a connection with one or more of your spiritual guides you may begin to receive what I like to call, an *energy signature*. This will be your guide's way of letting you know they are with you and close in your auric field (in your aura). Often this is a strange sensation somewhere on your body. However it may also be a vision, a flash of colour or a sound. Let me share with you my first experience with energy signatures when I was beginning to connect with Red Eagle;

It began for me after I dreamt of painting him. I was reading a lot and was learning how to meditate. When I would meditate (and sometimes when I wasn't), I would start to get this very strong pressure across my nose. Sometimes it was so strong that it felt like my face was twisting. After talking to some people with more experience in this area than I did at the time, I was still unsure what this was. Some said it was connected with my third eye chakra, however this never felt right me. It wasn't until several years later that I was able to recognise that it was Red Eagle's *energy signature*. So whenever he wants to come forward, or he wants me to know he is there, he lets me know with this energy signature.

Another example I will give you is from my spiritual surgeon. A spiritual surgeon is a being in spirit who comes through via your energy to perform surgeries on you or your clients (I will talk about spiritual surgery later in this book). When coming close to my body, my surgeon would lightly buzz in my left ear. This was his energy signature that let me know he was ready to work.

Let's call one of your spiritual guides forward and see if you can sense their energy signature.

Exercise (ii): Becoming aware of your spiritual guides

Make sure your body is nice and comfortable in the position that it's in. If it isn't then make a few adjustments.

When you are ready draw a nice and comfortable breath in, hold and breathe out, breathing all the air out of your body.

As you do this, feel your body become heavy on the chair or where you are, feel your weight and all parts of you connecting to what is under you (the floor, chair, earth etc).

Allow your gaze on these words to soften, and continue to breathe.

When you are ready, ask one of your spiritual guides to step close to you. Stop reading for a moment, as you open your entire aura and energy to sense this being's presence.

Take note of any sensations. These can include something like a pressure, coolness, etc. somewhere on your body, it may be a word or thought that pops into your mind or something visual you receive, like a daydream. This visual thing may be a flash of colour, or a vision of your guide next to you. It doesn't matter what your guide does as an energy signature, trust it as real and perfect for both of you. It cannot be wrong.

You thank your guide for bringing their signature to your attention, and you make a commitment to spend more time working with your spiritual guide in the future.

Gently bring your focus back to the room, and if you need to make notes of your experience, please do.

Your guides love connecting with you. However please always remember that unless it is an emergency, they cannot help you unless you ask them. My suggestion for you is to begin calling your guides into any task you do throughout your day. Ask them to help you find a car park in a certain place; if you are waiting to speak to a telephone operator ask your guides to help you get someone who is happy, helpful and friendly; to help you learn what you can during meditation; to help you find your lost keys; or to help you or your children sleep peacefully at night.

There are no limitations to what they can help you achieve, so please, I say this on behalf of your guides, ask them to help you.

If you require something more visual to connect with your guides, I recommend looking for a spiritual artist who can draw their interpretation of your spiritual guide. These drawings contain the essence of your guide.

Many people have emotional reactions to these drawings and feel they totally help them connect with their guides on a deeper level. You will find our contact details at the beginning or end of this book.

Trust in your spirit guide connection, know you have support and help if you choose to take it.

I have a lot to thank my spiritual guides for. My guides tell me that their role in my life is easy, because they can seed ideas into my heart and creative mind, and I take action eagerly. Because of this I have many guides working with me, and many lining up ready to connect as new ideas unfold.

For me, I always flow with what I am feeling, and in truth I know my spiritual guides are a part of me. I don't look outside myself to worship them or put unrealistic expectations onto them, or to even put them onto a pedestal. To me, we are all equal and have important roles to play equally. As a synergy we make a wonderful team. Our lives are potentially enhanced by this union and this connection with our 'inner community.'

'May your now be perfect and full of love, strength and abundance. May you find courage and confidence to face your life's challenges and turn them into opportunities.'

Lee-Anne Peters

Chapter 8 – Intuitive Energy Healing

I hadn't long been doing distant healings when the healing service 'Intuitive Energy Healing' emerged. I found this title covered everything that could possibly occur during a healing session.

You see, after many years of self healing and healing experience I discovered that it really doesn't matter what you 'do' in terms of healing and helping others.

Everything you read, learn and experience through your life's journey, contribute to the skills available to you for helping others. I also found that often what my clients or even I thought was needed, wasn't needed at all. And that there really was a higher presence out there, be it in the form of spiritual guides, higher self, or the creator who had a higher understanding of everything that had led the client to me. This knowledge and understanding was often beyond what either my client or myself understood.

So I quickly learnt to trust this higher guidance and open myself up, allowing spirit to do what was needed for my clients highest good.

In fact, over the past decade I have only participated in two courses, the rest of my skills come from self experience, books, talking to others and self healing. The first, spiritual surgery practitioner's course opened me up in the most amazing ways. And often this is what happens. Many people 'wake up' to this spiritual and colourful world due to an amazing course or life experience. I often describe it as waking up into a world of 'colour.' And when reflecting to the time before waking up, it seemed to have a 'black and white' hue.

Everything I do in my life brings with it a lesson or a valuable experience. This is why I regret nothing. I love where I am in my life, and it was every choice, decision and action I took in every moment past that has brought me to now. And for this I am always grateful. I have learnt to turn an apparent obstacle into an opportunity and you can do this too.

During one of my intuitive energy healing sessions, whether it is in person or via distance, spirit taps into my large experience pool.

This is what I love about intuitive healing, when you are fully open and trusting in the moment, and let go of every need to control, you allow everything to flow perfectly.

One of the most common things I do in my healing sessions is energy cleansing and balancing. So many people have energy systems that are out of balance and need a thorough clean out. This is where I 'run energy' through my client's energy body or auras & chakras. By 'running energy' I mean flushing out their system with light and energy. Similar to how we have a shower to cleanse our physical body, but in this case we soften the energy and work it throughout the whole body, including the emotional, mental and spiritual levels.

I often suggest to my clients and participants in my workshops that a great habit to get into is a daily energy cleanse. I suggest that when you are in the shower, you visualise or imagine the water running over your aura. Now your aura protrudes out from your physical body. There are many layers to the aura, and within the first layer, the layer closest to the physical body are a set of energy centres called the seven major chakras. I work with chakras a lot and I feel they hold very valuable information and insight as to why our body may be experiencing pain, discomfort or odd sensations. In the shower imagine the water running through your aura and chakras, clearing out all the toxins and old energy from there and washing them down the drain. Feel it all go, let everything go in that moment. Then imagine a 'plug' plugging at the soles of your feet and then shift the energy a little and begin to fill your body up with love, light or any other form of energy that feels right in the moment.

By doing this simple act everyday you cleanse and charge your energy. This is especially important for people who work daily helping or interacting with others. Also for people who are very sensitive to energy and seem to take on other people's 'pain.' Give it a try, adapt it to suit your needs and the flow of your body.

Distant Intuitive Healing details:

Below you will be able to read and connect with a distant *'Intuitive Energy Healing'* I did for a client from the United States. As you read these healing details, you may feel energy moving in your body, as if you are also experiencing this healing now for yourself. Trust your body and allow yourself to feel.

"Here is your intuitive energy healing. As with all my healing and reading work I connect with your energy and become sensitive to you, I will feel things within my body. As I know my body really well, I know what is not my feeling. I never take on other people's 'stuff' I use this as a way to connect and heal, that works for me. I will also hear messages and see visions. I will trust whatever I am shown and take action accordingly.

Let your healing begin...

I feel strongly drawn to work with three of my healing energy cards. I am drawn to cards #21 (third eye opening) and #13 (meditation) to help open your third eye chakra, and I also feel that we will work on trust for you, and help clear any trust blocks or issues that are stopping you from progressing further right now. I have a feeling that there is a substantial block that is blocking you from fully trusting your intuition. I will look more into this shortly.

The other card that jumped out for you now was #17 (time tunnels). To be drawn to this card suggests that there is work we will be doing involving past lives and karmic blocks that are holding you back.

I call on spirit fully now to connect deeply for your healing. I feel a heaviness in energy to the right side of your head, which seems to flow around to your right eye, and down the right side of your neck. There is a heavy pushing feeling and a sense of darkness. The darkness doesn't mean anything bad. The feeling is that it may be something that you avoid or deny thinking about or feeling. Or it may be a specific event or situation that has caused energy congestion there.

Spirit now directs me to do an energy cleanse on your system. This will help clear any surface energy residue and will assist us to access deeper levels for your healing.

Archangel Michael steps forward, he is standing tall and there is a sense of honour as he bows gently to you. He feels as honoured to be in your presence as you do with him. He is treating you with respect, compassion and equality.

He fiddles with the top of your head, at your crown chakra, for a few moments, and the feeling is that he is opening something 'up' for you. I hear him mutter a few commands, and he looks up above him. A beam of light gently pours down. It calmly flows into your crown chakra. Your crown chakra is your centre that helps you connect with the world beyond the physical. I feel it tingle here, as it opens deeply to this high energy light. The light now appears as a very soft gold. A gold that feels very balancing, calming and a very high vibration. It has like a 'white gold' appearance. The light flows and fills your crown and down into your entire head space. Every corner and area there is beginning to fill and shine with light. As it does this, it activates your third eye chakra. Which is your centre for intuition, vision and trust. I see this white gold light work into your third eye chakra from the inside out, as it beams a very powerful laser like beam of light out from your inner third eye. It beams out, far away from you, connecting you deep into where you need to be and who you need to be with for your highest good. This beam coming from here feels like an arm reaching forward into your future and into the heart of your love, and those who you require in your life in the coming future. Everything is perfect and as it is meant to be.

I see Archangel Michael now directs this beam of light into your throat chakra. This is your centre for expression, communication, truth and feeling safe to speak your truth. You open your mouth fully, allowing the light to work as deep into this area as possible. You surrender, relax and allow the light to work in the way it is needed for your highest good at this time. The light surrounds your neck also, highlighting it, and illuminating it with this overwhelming sense of compassion and love. With your mouth still wide open, you breathe a deep breath in and hold, then out, exhaling all the air from your body, and expressing this. Your throat makes a soft hissing noise as you do. With this you close your mouth and the energy flows down your spine to your heart chakra.

Your heart chakra, is your centre for love of self, others and all creation. This area is like a sponge and absorbs an overwhelming amount of this love. It begins to gently spin, and rotate, absorbing all the love it needs now. There is a strong sense of green energy here. Which is suggesting that you either have a healing or helping heart, or that your heart or the love area of your life is growing and healing right now. For me, the truth feels that a bit of both is occurring. Your heart continues to open and widen and take all the energy it needs. This is also distributed out through all your arteries and veins into your body, along with your cells, nervous system and every connection that is made to your heart, blood and your life system. Your heart begins to shine in this beautiful light.

The light now expands and continues to flow down your spine to your solar plexus chakra, which is just above your navel and is your centre for personal power, strength and courage. Here the light gently works into this area. There is a feeling that this centre for you, is quite active, and it is eased and calmed by the light. Other energies for this chakra are that it is yellow, and it represents your masculine self. It can often appear like a golden sun on your belly. This is where you receive your drive and Will to do certain things. The energy here is very active and raw, and the light adds a sense of feminine energy to it, this will help with balance. Still allowing you to do the things that you enjoy, yet bringing about more harmony to this specific area. The light fills into your organs around your upper stomach, working through and into exactly where it is needed. Your solar plexus, and surrounding areas expand with this calming love, as the light flows down to your sacral chakra, which is just below your navel and is your centre for emotional, sexual and creative energies. This also represents your feminine self and the lunar energies. There is a deep sense of balance here. I feel that deeply this is balanced, but there are a few surface blocks that have come up recently or are about to. The light flows all around this area, moving deeply into your stomach. All bodily functions and organs here are being filled and flushed with the light.

The light continues to flow down to your base chakra, which is at the base of your spine and is your centre for survival instincts and grounding. Here the golden light fills and helps clear any blocks within this chakra. The light also works around through your reproductive system and all areas around the base of your spine. This whole area begins to glow with calming loving light.

The golden light flows down your legs and out your feet into the earth beneath you. This is helping strengthen your connection with earth and will help anchor you into the moment. The more grounded and anchored we are, the more this helps propel us into the universe for a more powerful and deeper experience.

Now the golden light flows back up your legs, up your spine, flushing your whole spine out, and the light shoots up out of the top of your head and into your aura. Helping clear any debris or foreign energy within it.

I breathe deeply, and feel your energy now, I am shown the vision of a bridge, and a need to bridge the gap between one world and the next, between this world and the next world, between male and female, between earth and sky, black and white, giving and receiving, in and out. The bridge represents that aspect of balance. That perfect space in between the opposites, that which also contains each opposing side. The pendulum swings from one to the other, until we find this bridge that brings harmony and balance to the polarity. One side must not be favoured more than the other, this is what creates the imbalance, it must all be treated and accepted as equal. As being in harmony, when this occurs, you will find that space of silence in between the breath. That space that contains an equal amount of 'in' and 'out' breath; that space in between your heart beats; that space of sacred silence. Within this silence is much wisdom, for when we look and feel the balance within, this teaches more than what one learns whilst living in the swinging from one pole to the other.

With this wisdom, and another deep breath, I feel your energy calm, cool and relax. We are now ready to go deeper with your healing.

Archangel Michael steps back slightly, but remains here right now.

There is a strong feeling that your third eye needs activating, this may be blocks with your intuition, it may also be a trust block, or something deeper, and that is embedded within your DNA. Your master DNA gland is held deep within your third eye chakra in your pineal gland. As I type this now, I feel my third eye chakra begin to spin very quickly, this occurs as I become sensitive to your energy for your healing.

I feel a very high and powerful spiritual being step forward. He calls himself the 'I Am'. He doesn't feel necessarily male, but to gender-ise him, 'he' is most appropriate. I feel that he represents a high aspect of yourself, your 'I AM'. Your 'all that I am.'

I see this grand and powerful being stand before you, he bows in honour of you, and then lifts his right index finger, and slowly points it to your third eye chakra. As it gets closer I see clearly a beam of white light leaving his finger tip and moving into your third eye.

As this is occurring I feel that earlier when I saw the beam of light exiting your third eye, that this beam was going forward and not only calling forward other people to you, but also your 'I AM', he heard the call and came forward for your highest good.

As this activation is taking place, I am feeling quite high energies within my body (which reflects your body), I feel a very high tingling on the crown chakra, which usually happens with very high energy vibrations. I also feel a tingling feeling going down your spine from the top down, and stopping at the back aspect of your solar plexus. The tingling is very strong at the back aspect of your heart.

Your 'I AM's' finger is now almost touching your third eye chakra. While the finger is here, I feel energy moving in your sacral chakra, also your third eye is very active.

He now very lightly touches his finger onto your third eye chakra, and with this, there is a strong feeling and vision of a very high electric or energy charge running throughout your body. It is so powerful and intense. I stretch your body to help anchor this light into your being. I can feel the light flood into all areas of your being, bringing forward a feeling of heaviness / tiredness, as your body moves past this, and truly surrenders. Use your breath now - breathe in deeply, and as you breathe out, hiss and let all the air and sound out from your throat (the back of heart is tingling very strongly now). As you do this, feel your body surrender, release and truly let go. Feel it become heavy, yet light at the same time. Any tightness within your body, become aware of it, feel it, and then breathe into that tightness and surrender the tightness to this moment.

The power of this energy beam of light is almost indescribable in earth words. Words that come to mind, which still limit the energy in a lot of ways, are love, light, acceptance, change, spring, growth, activation, white, all knowing, all loving, all compassionate and all BE ing.

I now search closer 'into' your third eye, I feel that there are specific details that need to now be described to you in greater detail. The source of the light, which is entering at your third eye chakra, is highly illuminating this area. It is glowing with light, which is bright, but not blinding. I adjust my eyes, and look within the bright light. Within here I see a bean, which is a seed. It is tiny, but I feel I am looking at it through some sort of magnifying lens. The seed has been there since your creation, since the creation of your soul itself. It is an ancient seed that has been surrounded in this golden glow since the dawn of your time. It is now the right time for this seed to be activated, and set alight! The beam of light is deeply penetrating this seed. This seed which stores all memories, all energies and all destinies of you as a being. That which you have long forgotten is coming to the forefront of your memory. That which has long been holding you back from being your truest self, is waking up.

The seed stirs, the seed awakens, it begins to sprout and grow. I would call this seed, a 'golden seed', just because it is bathing within the gold, and as it sprouts, I continue to see this golden aura around it.

This activation will take some time to work fully through your body, and into the seed. So as this continues to occur within you, spirit wants me to talk with you about something else, something sacred, a deep, deep memory within you.

We are travelling back in time (with assistance from spirit and Healing Energy Card #17 - time tunnels) the location is hot and fairly sandy. The buildings around are old, they are poorly made, and blend with the landscape. There are a lot of poor people around, but I also sense that the opposite is true over the hill, where people live well. These are simple times, yet they are times which change the course of the future, they change the course of belief for the many, and here many seeds within are planted. This is in Jerusalem during the time of Christ. I sense that there is a beautiful connection here for you, one which is getting close to needing your remembering.

The people were just normal people, nothing special, just their own unique selves. There was an ever present internal and often external conflict between the poor and the wealthy. The religious and the non-religious. The great divide was evident here in many ways and forms. For people and even when you look or feel the energy of the town, there was a great divide between everything. The energy and area was separated.

The man they called Jeshua, would often walk on the side of the poor, helping them feel powerful and loved. He was a gentle soul, one of deep compassion, one who shined hope to those in need, yet someone who was also one of them. Even though after his death he was put on a pedestal, in truth and in his actions he was no different to the plain commoner.

Where do you fit in this picture? Well, you watched this happen, you were the great observer. The observer who learned so much from this experience. You were the old man who was homeless, you spent a lot of time on the corner, with a few other homeless people. Here you saw all the actions and were in many ways 'hidden' from the involvement of the situations. It was like often people thought you were just another brick in the wall, you didn't have much impact on the world there, but, your role was extremely important. You were the great observer. The one who didn't speak, but did a lot of listening. Jeshua walked past you and stopped, and noticed you many times on his local journeys. This filled your heart. For many years, you were sad, and wore the pressures of the world on your shoulders, but with a few simple words of compassion and love from this generous soul, you changed your view. In fact your whole outlook and internal feeling began to change.

You began to notice that people seemed to change, because you had internally. The world looked a lot brighter, you felt brighter, you were exactly where you needed to be. You can close your eyes now and feel or see what you saw in those times. Take yourself back there, imagine that you are that old toothless man on the corner, and notice what you see. What do you witness? What do you feel that changes who you are forever? Spend as much time as you need doing this. If you have trouble, just use your imagination, and trust your first impression or what you feel. Listen to your body, and make notes if you need to.

I breathe deeply, feeling your memories firmly anchor into your being, into your heart. The feeling is compassion, love and truth.

I am now drawn to your third eye chakra, and I notice that this internal 'seed' has begun to sprout in an amazing way. It has three firm and strong sprouts, with budding leaves opening. The roots are anchoring gently into your body and the seed itself is beginning to split and bring life within you. There is a strong DNA connection here too. A DNA activation; an awakening of deep cellular memories within. This is all linked.

With the energy still strong, but the feeling of the beam is subsiding, your body is full now of this powerful light. I see and feel the energy merge with your expanded heart chakra; the two memories, that have been deeply embedded are merging into one great love. Two separates unite. Two poles balance and combine. What was once torn apart is now One. The great merging of the left and right, the male and female is taking place.

This is a huge energy to occur within you. This is where you begin to truly feel whole and complete. Enjoy and bathe in this united love.

I work now on your breath. Breathing this love and Oneness all around your body, as every cell is graced with both aspects of the opposite, which bring a powerful feeling of being One. Every cell is touched with aspects of light and dark, all that was opposite, is now in harmony.

Start to really notice all the balances around you. That space in between the poles. Especially in nature.

Your I AM now smiles with you, and bows his head in respect for you, as he steps forward and merges within you. He is an aspect of your true self.

Archangel Michael, who has been witnessing and helping hold this energy space, now gives you a gentle wave and steps back into the light.

I scan your energy, and your vibration is extremely high. You are glowing from the inside out, in perfect balance.

We anchor this healing, and these high vibrations into your body by imagining the roots of this seed moving deeply down through your body and down through the soles of your feet and into the earth below you. See and feel these roots weave and embed the essence of your being into the earth, around rocks, and holding on tight and firmly to the inner earth. You are nice and firmly planted into the earth and into the moment.

This healing has affected many levels of your being on extremely deep and also not so deep levels. I can feel this is having a physical, emotional, mental and spiritual effect for you.

The energy begins to subside, and the feeling of change within is amazing, beyond words."

If you felt energy moving as you read and connected with this healing, please use the power of your breath to breathe that old energy out and away from you, and to draw the new energy 'in' through the power of your 'in' breath. And please drinks lots of nice refreshing water to help that old energy move through your body. Again, trust and listen to your body and what it feels it needs in this moment.

Everyone's healing session is different and unique and manifests according to my client's energy in that moment. This means that I know and trust that whatever occurs is for my client's highest good. I step away from my ego, my mind and any desire I may have in wanting to control what is to happen, and I completely surrender and allow my intuition and my guides to flow through me. This allows for a freely flowing Divine healing to take place, an Intuitive Energy Healing!

Chapter 9 – Healing with colour

My interest in drawing and art began during my 4th year of school in 1985. I quickly realised that I could fairly easily draw anything I could see. My interest in art turned into a passion once I entered high school in 1988. I had several amazing art teachers whom I loved working with. I began to love using charcoal, pastels and acrylic paint. I studied visual arts a little in college (which are years 11 & 12 where I went to school), however I found the compulsory subject of art theory incredibly boring, so I didn't take it any further; I just dabbled with it at home.

When I began studying hairdressing in 1994, my hairdressing teacher told me that I was in the wrong profession and that I should in fact be an artist. At the time for me, I lacked confidence to pursue art, so I continued to make a hobby out of it. Hairdressing was essential in my development; I learnt a great many skills that would help me get Temple of Balance off the ground. I learnt about the importance of great customer service, how to work under pressure, how to communicate with my clients and how to help them feel good. But in regards to art, hairdressing taught me confidence. I was developing more personal power and understanding about who I was and what I wanted in life.

Between leaving college in 1993 and consciously beginning my spiritual journey in 2001, I created a few of my own personal art projects around my home, including dragon murals and other drawings usually of landscapes and sunsets. I also did a few tattoo designs and some artwork for my father's fruit and vegetable shop. I still loved creating art, but only ever saw it as a hobby.

The moment I awakened spiritually, I began to draw spirit guides. It began with the Indian I dreamed of and my own guides, then it evolved into guide drawing for others several years before I started Temple of Balance. I would draw a spirit guide as it presented itself to me, and then I would frame it and put it for sale in my father's shop. The right person would come along and purchase it. I had no idea who was buying it, but I felt excited that my work was selling!

My spiritual guide, Red Eagle was a huge influence with my art, and I knew that this was part of my purpose. Soon after Temple of Balance was founded I began to list spirit guide drawings for sale on eBay, I had a steady number of orders coming in from around the world and in 2007 I began to see the real potential art had in healing.

A lady asked me if I would draw her a picture to help her lose weight. I wasn't sure what to do, but I cleared my ego out of the way, removed all thoughts and just flowed with my intuition. I created an orange / yellow, five pointed star (You can see this as Healing Energy Card; 5. Self Acceptance). Within the star were various symbols and around the star was outer space, blackness filled with stars. I thought I would experiment to see how affective art was for healing. So I set up a small group of different people from around the world and presented this drawing I had done for 'weight loss.' I didn't tell them who I had drawn it for or why I had drawn it, I just told them that it was for healing and asked if they would work closely with the drawing for a week to see if anything affected them.

The reports were very interesting. Three out of the five thought I had drawn it specifically for them, they felt a strong connection to it. And several reported some weight loss and changes in eating habits once I announced what my intention was for this drawing. One lady reported to me that every week when she went to the sports field she would buy something unhealthy from the kiosk, but when she started working with the drawing she felt no urge to do it. This astounded me and this was the beginning of my Healing Energy Cards.

I began to experiment and work more with healing art and over a few months had enough drawings to create a pack of Healing Cards. A lot of people were stuck and needed help and there was only so much I could do, and only so many people I could help every day from my computer. I felt that I had to create some tools so that people could help themselves. Before I had the first thirty two Healing Energy Cards printed into a pack, I worked with the samples every day. Using them with clients during distant healing sessions and also on myself.

When I felt the time had come to look at getting them printed and out into the world I looked at a few options. To get them printed and published from a publishing company never felt right to me. So I saved my money and had five hundred packs printed at a local printing warehouse. Orders came in quickly along with reports of amazing healings and miracles that the cards facilitated. The first self published pack was released in 2008. Now I had some tools to offer my clients for self healing, and this I was very pleased with. I am passionate about empowering others to heal themselves; for me, I feel this is the way it should be.

In mid 2009 my husband and I were lucky enough to sit next to a very special woman on a plane trip. It was by no accident that our seats were matched. Jane was sitting at the window seat and was reading a workbook that clearly showed subtle energy, chakras and auras. After a few minutes I couldn't help myself and I asked her about what she was reading. With hesitation she began to explain, I quickly reassured her that both my husband and I were healers. Relief swept across her beautiful face as a connection between the three of us was instantly built. Jane was like a sponge drawing in everything we were sharing and saying, and we got onto the subject of my Healing Energy Cards. She was very excited, and being a well known and active positive psychologist in Sydney she was eager to begin using them with her clients. Jane loved my cards and sent me many reports of success and how she liked to use them in her sessions.

There are so many different ways to work with the cards, and one thing I just love about them is that they evolve with us. So it doesn't matter what energy 'space' we are in, as we grow, heal, let go and expand our energy vibration, the cards continue to reflect to you what you need for your healing and growth.

It wasn't long after I founded Temple of Balance that I found out that I could easily see, draw and heal the aura and chakras for people via distance. Again, this was another huge awakening for me, as I didn't need to 'see' the person right in front of me to 'see' their aura. All I needed to do was 'think of' or 'tune into' the person and I would begin to 'see.' It was quite incredible. And quickly my distant service of Aura & Chakra Colour healing & drawing became quite popular for clients. I couldn't believe how accurate they were. I would just flow and create what I felt, relay messages, feelings and guidance back to clients via email, and would send a scanned copy of how I saw their aura, and they would be amazed. Many couldn't believe that I would 'know them' better and deeper than they knew themselves. I also found that parents loved to order this service for their children. I feel it is because children often struggle to communicate or put into words how they feel. And it was invaluable for parents to see how another saw their child's energy and what effects certain things were having on them.

One of the most common visions I would see in auras during this service was the total lack of energy down the legs. And the interesting thing was that most of people's energy was stuck around their heads!

To me, the area of the aura around the head I call the mind energy. The mind energy consists of thoughts, ideas, worries, stresses, fears, joy and anything else stored in the mind. Because in these current times people are spending so much time worrying and thinking it is creating a lot of excess energy around the head, which then depletes the lower areas of the body. If you can imagine these thoughts appearing as energy or colour, and every time you think a worrying, negative or destructive thought, its heavy energy hovers around your head. If you think these thoughts or negative and destructive thoughts a lot of the time through the day, then over a period of time this creates a pressure or weight over the head. Sometimes when I am doing a healing for a client, and they have been thinking this way for a long period of time, I begin to get a headache or feel pressure over my head as I become sensitive to my client during the healing session. The intenseness for me, depends on how consistent or how 'time consuming' the negative thoughts of my clients are.

Our thoughts are so important. What we think or believe creates the world we live in. To think negative or destructive thoughts over time will begin to affect your body. Please start to become more aware of what you are thinking and saying. Ask yourself if these thoughts mirror your highest intentions for yourself. Do they mirror your truth? You are the only one who can get back in control of your mind and what you are thinking. Meditation can help you with this and I will talk more about meditation a bit later.

Several years ago when I began to realise that I wasn't thinking constructive / productive thoughts I started to pay attention to my thoughts and words more. I noticed how people reacted to what I said, and also how I reacted to what I said and if those words really were aligned with my truth. I began to consciously change what I was thinking and saying, and this changed my life. Because I started to see that every thought had energy and if that thought was negative or destructive then it had a corresponding affect on me, I imagined that each of my thoughts were written in the sky for everyone to see. That they weren't hidden within me, locked away in a secret compartment only for me to know about. But in fact they had affects that either manifested in my body or in my life.

When I see this concentrated energy around the heads of those I draw for I notice that when so much energy is focused there it actually draws energy out of the body, which is why not many people have much energy around their lower half. This then usually manifests for the person as a constant tiredness or feeling of being drained. In fact, that is what's happening. The mind is draining the body of energy to survive on a daily basis. So in my healing work and also my aura & chakra drawings, I spend a lot of time lightening the area of the mind energy and directing energy back down into the body. We call this process, grounding. You may have heard of this before, but maybe it isn't clear to you exactly what 'being grounded' is. Well, to be grounded is to be present in the moment. It is also when our body has a nice even and balanced flow of energy, and it is not too 'top heavy' with negative mind thoughts.

Have you ever thought about a connection with thinking and how fast time seems to go sometimes? Well, the more we think, think and think some more, the faster time goes. Why is this? Well, because when lots of energy is hovering in the mind energy thinking about what needs to be done tomorrow, worrying about what might happen next week or having trouble moving forward from the past. When every moment is consumed with this thinking away from the now, then it actually makes time 'appear' to speed up.

When we are grounded and our energy is nice and balanced in our body and our negative thinking has settled down, time actually begins to slow.

Consider this for a moment... draw a nice relaxing breath, really feel the air as it enters your nose or mouth, feel your body draw that breath in through each muscle in your lungs and diaphragm. Now hold this breath for a moment, and listen for your heartbeat, how are your toes feeling? How about your stomach and legs? And on the out breath feel your body release and let the old air out. Feel your muscles relax, feel your body sink deeper where you are.

Now how many moments have passed by? Consider a time recently when you were worrying or thinking a lot, how quickly did time go then compared to just now?

So much time is wasted on worrying and negative destructive thinking. Please don't waste another moment. Turn those negative thoughts into positive ones. Draw that heavy energy from the mind energy down into your body by doing things that are grounding and help anchor you in the here and now.

There are lots of ways to stay grounded. Here are some ideas:

- Focus on the power of your breathing.
- Spend time in nature, and pay attention to everything around you there.
- Exercise, walk and move your body.
- Spend time with like-minded people who are positive and you feel safe to be around.
- Household chores are very grounding. When you do these, if you can pay attention to your body. Watch your arm as you sweep the floor.
- Laugh, create and have fun in the moment.
- Spend good quality time with you. Nurturing and nourishing yourself is very important and will help you be more positive towards yourself and others.
- Self healing time; where you imagine grounding energy, maybe in the form of tree like roots that move from the soles of your feet and embed you deeply down into the Earth and into the now.
- Some crystals are very grounding too. Some examples are red jasper, black tourmaline and

tiger's eye. We will talk more about the healing power of crystals shortly.

You may have noticed that many of these grounding suggestions are very physical. That is because being physical is being present in the here and now. If you love where you are in your life now, if you are truly happy and you are not dreaming of a better life or a life like someone else, then you will remain grounded and balanced.

If you aren't happy now and your heart doesn't sing, ask yourself why. And also ask yourself what can you do to change this? No matter how much you may feel another person is to blame, in truth it is only you who can make changes. You may be waiting on the other person for the rest of your life; do you want to be miserable for that amount of time? Change can be challenging, however change is natural and when we flow in synchronicity with our heart's desire and what is right and positive for us, then we flow into happiness and wholeness. No one deserves to suffer or be in emotional, mental or physical pain. What can you do to change what is happening in your life?

Not only is it important to be aware of your thoughts, but also to take action to change negative or unwanted thoughts. Stop yourself in the thought stage when you think something judgmental, negative or something that isn't aligned with your highest truth. Halt it there and replace the thought with something positive.

In general, changes can happen at any time in our life, expected or unexpected. If we commit to changing our mind thoughts then action must be taken. Change won't come about from just talking about it. Change comes from taking positive and productive steps that bring you out of the habit. To change your experience then you must change the habit. What habits have you gotten yourself into? These can include physical toxic habits, but also habits of thought, habits of things you do every day and so on. These everyday habits may have become little ritual type things, where you probably don't even give it much thought. Maybe something you 'have to do' or have 'always done' at certain times of the day. Pay attention and notice these habits and I challenge you to break the 'need' of them. Maybe try doing them at a different time of the day or in a different way. Step out of the rut and flow with change.

Having dark colours like black or red in the aura are not a bad thing from my perspective. I find black a very positive colour. Black is very protective and is also a colour of change, new beginnings and depth. Many people I have met over the years are very 'anti' black. Even my son's kindergarten teacher despised black so much that she removed all the black textas (markers) from the colouring pots. There seem to be a lot of old religious superstitions associated with black. And the thing you must ask yourself is what black means to you. Place all of that old conditioning and what you have been 'told' by others aside. How does the colour black make you feel? Does it feel like the unknown and a little fearful? If it does for you, this is actually a very common reaction to black. So instead of resisting dealing with this colour and the fear of the unknown, why not energetically turn and face it and look into the blackness. Find the courage within to face your fears, to overcome any obstacle. Cast your fears aside and break the habits, break down those old conditions and what you believe about things based on what you have been told as a child, on the television or even by people you look up to. Don't believe anything; instead feel in your heart and body for the truth. If it feels right then take it on, if it doesn't then cast it aside. Sometimes we feel something is true for us, but then later in our life, due to our life experience, that belief is challenged. It is okay to change your views, to change your beliefs and truth. Self reflect and discover what is your truth, what do you do out of habit and what do you do out of joy. For me, I don't see any change as bad or negative, my approach to change is that it is an opportunity. An opportunity for me to grow, learn and evolve into a better and happier me.

A common thing to see in the aura is emotional blockages. I find some people focus so much energy and time into these emotions, that not only are they intertwined with their mind thoughts, but they present themselves as an energy block in the body. I may see this as a blob or ball of heaviness around their stomachs, shoulders or throat. Where the block is in the body gives us little clues to help us understand about the emotional block. The more emotions entangled in the block, the more emotional I feel as I become sensitive to my client's energy. I never take their energy on, I just become sensitive to them for their healing, and the moment the healing is over I have all of my energy back.

If there is an energy block that is full of emotion around or near the throat then this usually indicates that the person is 'choked up' or is finding it difficult to share how they feel through their expressions. You see, the throat chakra is your centre for communication, expression and truth, but also feeling safe to speak your truth. We are often faced with people in our lives that we don't feel completely comfortable to be ourselves around and in turn we often don't say what we need to say. Over a long period of time this builds up in the energy system or aura as an energy block. Eventually this energy block, if left unchecked, may lead to physical symptoms or disease can set in.

The aura and chakras can reveal a lot about what is going on behind the scenes for a person. My aim is to continue teaching others like you, how to become sensitive to your aura and chakras and how to transfer what you are seeing or feeling onto paper. Ultimately it is about us, working on ourselves, trying things out for ourselves and then expanding our personal experience and knowledge into helping others, if that is your calling. Whether you are here to help others or not is up to you, but I still feel that we all can get back in touch with our true essence by practising self reflection, self awareness and getting back in tune with our intuition.

Chapter 10 – Karmic Patterns

Early on in my conscious spiritual and healing journey I read a book called 'Essential Energy Balancing' by Diane Stein. This book opened me up to the world of karmic patterns, fears and illusions that hold us back in our life. This book totally resonated with me and I began to immediately bring what I was learning into my self-healing. I began to recognise embedded fears and patterns I was carrying within my body. This old hurt and pain was coming to the surface in my life.

I looked into separation issues, I had that covered with my parents separating and actually this separation issue went right back to deaths I had in past lives and separation from my home in the stars. At this particular time in my life I was experiencing separations everywhere around me, but it took me a little while to recognise what was actually going on behind the scenes. Situations where playing out, these situations didn't feel related at the time of the drama, however through a lot of self healing I have learnt to see the bigger picture.

Let's go back to the source of these 'karmic patterns.' Let's use a situation connected with an old fear I used to carry with me. Now a long time ago, in fact it was a whole other lifetime in another body, I watched a dear friend of mine burn at the stake, just prior to me burning. This left a scar within me. A scar that in this lifetime, manifested as a deep fear of fire. Early in this lifetime I dreamt about fire chasing me and due to the location of my childhood home and my bedroom window, I actually watched several houses burn to the ground. Now this fear wasn't present in my life every moment, but sometimes due to a dream, watching or hearing about something the fear and feelings associated with it came to the surface again for me. Then one day I was reading a book, and in my body I could feel emotions rising, so I retreated to my bedroom for some quiet time. Here I asked to be shown the 'source' of what I was feeling. And in my mind, as a vision, I saw myself watching my friend burning at the stake. This bought up so much emotion for me, watching this in my mind, feeling it in my body and experiencing it again. However this time was different, I actually got to see and experience the source of my fear and I had learnt how to release and let go, and this I did. I have now released and healed my fear of fire. I know I have healed this because very soon after and to this moment, I don't have the emotions and reactions around 'fire' like I used to.

What I learnt is that in a past life an 'injury' occurred on some level. Whether it is emotional, mental, physical or spiritual it doesn't matter. That trauma created a 'wound.' Now our soul being pure, wise and all knowing, seeks to present scenarios to us so that we can heal and let that pain go. This in turn raises our energy vibration out of pain and into love and freedom. This is what our soul seeks for our body.

A way you may be able to relate to this is if you reflect back on your life and you recognise things that seem to 'happen' to you over and over. For example; the same partners, neighbours, co-workers, rejection, disappointment, failure etc. What is important with these karmic patterns isn't the person involved or the situation, but to look at the bigger picture and recognise the reactions that are stirred within you from those people or that situation. Do you seem to attract people into your life who reject you for example? Well when you take the people out of the equation, you are left with the feeling and reaction. So simply put, you have rejection issues. These rejection issues continue to present themselves in your life so you can heal and break that pattern. A couple of years ago, when healing times were much longer and the energy was denser, we would have to go back to the source of the pattern to then be allowed to release the pain. However, due to time speeding up and the energy vibration of the earth and people rising, healings and releases are virtually instant. These days all you may need to do is step outside the drama, see what your reactions are for what they are, listen to your body and understand what the core issue is for you. Is it rejection, abandonment, separation, disconnection etc?

When you discover what the core pattern is, then you can do some releasing and reprogram your mind thoughts and beliefs so you don't set yourself up for that lesson anymore. So learn everything you can.

I will share some ways to release that may work for you.

Breathing to release

One of the simplest ways to release is by working with the power of your breath. The great thing about breath releasing is that you can do it anywhere and in any situation. Let's do a little breathing / releasing exercise...

Exercise (iii): Releasing through your breath

Allow your gaze on these words to soften, and pay attention to your body making sure it is comfortable in the position that it's in, if it isn't, then make a few adjustments.

Bring your complete awareness to your body, feeling for any tension, pain, discomfort, which can be physical, emotional or mental. What is your current big concern in your life? What just doesn't seem to be working for you right now? Consider this situation, and as you consider it in your mind, pay attention to your body, become sensitive to it, and feel where you are 'holding' this present 'concern' within your body... take your time...

When you feel ready, gently switch your focus to your breath. Feel the air as it flows into your body via your nostrils or your mouth... follow your breath as it travels inside. Feel that new air enter inside you as it carries the oxygen around to all of the cells in your body.

As you prepare for your out breath, feel the change in direction, that moment between your in and out breath. Hold it for as long as is comfortable for you. As you breathe out now, feel all of that 'old' air leaving your body. Feel it carry away your present concerns and worries. Feel it all leaving you now.

You can force this old air out if you feel deeply affected by things going on in your life at this time. Exhale all the air from your body.

Breathing 'in' the new air and breathing 'out' the old air. Breathing 'in' the new and true and breathing 'out' your pain and suffering.

Know you can't do anything wrong here, you trust the flow of your 'in' and 'out' breath, trust in your body and get back in touch with your intuition.

Feel the power of your breath as it flows within your body.

Creative expression to release

Often we have so much mental and emotional energy stored within our bodies. This can in turn affect our physical body as the energy settles into the joints and organs. Sometimes, especially with children it can be difficult to put into words how we are feeling and this is where using creative expression can be very helpful. At most of my teaching events and when I am working with children, I have some mandala sheets handy for us to colour. Mandala colouring is very relaxing and healing. We can use the power of our intentions to create and release anything that is stored or stuck within our body, mind or emotions.

You can hold the intention to get out of your mind something you are worrying about. Imagine with every stroke of colour you add you are letting those worries go.

Alternatively, you may like to use mandala colouring to help manifest your dreams or desires. All you need to do is hold that intention in your actions and your mandala colouring will help you get those ideas and inspirations out of your mind and onto paper, thus helping your dream manifest and take form in the physical world.

You can find mandala templates to print and colour on the internet very easily. Why not give it a try and see if it works for you? If you want to take it another step further, why not start with a blank piece of paper, find something circular to trace around, or use a compass, and start creating your own mandala. They are extremely fun to focus on.

Moving your body to release

Over a long period of time, our unexpressed emotions or mental challenges (i.e. fears, worries stresses) stay stored within us. In this case they settle down into the body, usually being held in the bones, muscles or organs.

Our body is a very sensitive instrument and when we become sensitive and listen to it, it can help reveal areas where we are blocked or stagnant in our life. If you are literally feeling blocked or stuck, like there is something you want or need to do, but you don't know what it is. Then I highly recommend doing some body moving. This can be anything from a brisk walk, jogging, exercise, yoga, dancing etc. Even a few times a day having a body shake. Focusing and loosening every part of your body.

When you have some private time, you may like to put your favourite piece of uplifting music on and have a dance and twirl. Feel the freedom within every movement you make. Feel your body become alive.

Journal writing to release

Ever since my very first conscious spiritual experience I have been journal writing. In my journal I write about my day, how I felt, any observations I made about myself. Along with my meditations, healing experiences and things that stood out for me. I write poetry in my journal quite often. Also if I have done a card reading for myself, I always add it into my journal so I can reflect on it at a later time.

For me, I write in my journal every couple of days. However, if I am going through a challenging time, then I may write in it several times a day to help me sort things out and work out what is happening subliminally under the surface.

I also love journal writing because a few months or years later you can reflect back and see just how far you have come.

So you are not limited at all by what you write or do in your personal journal. It is for you to express and work out what is happening for you. You can purchase blank & lined note books for a couple of dollars in most multi-purpose shops. Maybe this will work for you and help you release your old hurt and pain, you won't know until you give it a go.

Healing cards / oracle cards for guidance & release

You will find many different guidance cards around in book stores or metaphysical shops. As far as which specific pack/s you require, this will be of personal choice.

Some oracle cards are great for one or two card selections and others for full readings. These are wonderful in giving us guidance that we need in the moment. They can offer insight, a different perspective and if you get the same card or cards often, then they are trying to tell you something.

With card reading, it always works on the basis of like attracts like. So with clear intentions, you will select the card or cards you require in that moment. Trust your inner guidance. Sometimes the words on the card don't resonate with us in that moment and sometimes they do. Sometimes the picture or the card title might resonate more for us. When you allow your energy to guide you to what feels right then you are trusting your intuition, and thus getting the guidance that you need from the cards. Please don't feel that all the words must mean something to you at the time. As you read, open your heart and your energy and get in tune with your body. Experiment with them and go with the flow.

In 2008 I transformed some of my healing artwork into a pack of Healing Energy Cards. I will talk more in depth about them a little later, however, these cards can be extremely helpful when we need to let go of things that just no longer work for us.

Intuitively select your Healing Energy Card and trust what you feel you would like to do with it to help you heal and release. Meditate, place it under your pillow, or lie down and place the card on your body so you can receive the healing vibrations.

Letter writing for release

This is an extremely powerful way to release, however I must stress and will continue to stress that it is essential that you DO NOT send any letter of release to a person you may be writing it to.

If you are feeling angry towards someone in your life, it doesn't matter who it is or what they have 'done,' the important thing is that you feel hurt and you feel blocked by this person's actions. Maybe there are a few other people who have made you feel like this too. Whatever the situation is for you, you may benefit from writing a letter to the person you feel emotions towards. Even if this person has passed away or you don't see them, it doesn't matter. This includes any person or individual who you feel anger or emotion towards.

In this letter you can address it to their name, and then let it all out. Write down how angry you are, how you feel, how they let you down or disappointed you. Write down anything and everything you feel you need to say. Cry, release, remember, and allow the anger to be expressed for you. As you get towards the end of the letter you may notice the intenseness of the emotions subsiding a bit for you. This is a great sign that you have released a lot.

On completion of your letter it will be important that you take steps to release the energies. The writing, remembering and feeling was you acknowledging and expressing how you feel.

To release the energy now, in the form of the letter there are a few things you can do, depending on where you are and what feels right for you in that moment.

You can burn the letter, knowing that the fire and smoke is carrying your burden away, releasing it from your body, mind and emotions.

You may like to place it in an envelope and post it. **Please note:** do not put any name on the front of the envelope. You will not receive any release or peace from sending it to the person, or even re-reading it. It will just keep the drama and energy going, so please, keep any envelope blank! As you post it, feel that old pain releasing and letting go with the letter, feel your freedom.

Ripping up your letter and throwing it out or casting it to sea, is another great way to release this old pain.

There are many methods and I trust something I have shared will work for you. Of course you may feel drawn to something not listed and if so, please honour your intuition and take the steps needed for release.

Cry, express and trust your intuition to release

Allow yourself to feel, cry and go with the flow. This will be a personal thing for you and sometimes different ways of release are necessary depending on whether the block is held in the physical, emotional or mental aspects of your being. Also depending on where you are, what is going on for you in that moment and how you are feeling.

If things seem so hard for you that you really can't see a way out and life just seems to pile more and more heavy stones onto you, please know that there is help available for you. At Temple of Balance we are always here to help and support you. So please check out our website, find the 'help me' page and see if you feel better once connecting. If you still feel very stuck, please email and share anything you feel. We never take on anyone's energy, so offloading to someone who listens and empathises with you may be helpful to you. You may also find help with local energy healers or meditation circles. Ask for help and pay attention for signs and guidance that may be leading you to a certain person or group near you. There is so much help out there and it doesn't need to cost you a fortune. Many healers will even do an exchange, so ask and communicate any concerns you may have. You are not alone, you can and are getting through this. Believe in your recovery, healing and freedom.

I AM Goddess, I dance & shine.

I AM full of life, there is no need to hide.

I step out from my hiding place, and up to the door.

I let go of the past, I commit to it all.

I step through it now, with eagerness and excitement.

I AM woman, I AM Goddess, I love being ME!

Lee-Anne Peters

Karmic release request – for deep releasing

For deeper releasing; like fears, very old wounds, or things that just feel so heavy and traumatic. Try this: *(Which is modified from Diane Stein's Karmic release request – Essential Energy Balancing book 1)*

This is what I request when I am working with myself or clients and when the 'wound' or old pain is very deep. I find it helps bring the old energy to the surface and then release it. See how it feels for you. I would only do this request when I felt the old energy rise to just below the surface. You can say something like this. Read through it first before you try, just to be sure it resonates with you.

Exercise (iv): Karmic release request

Work out what your core issue is, let's say for this exercise it is fear of rejection.

Call forward the Lords of Karma. Feel or know their presence is with you.

Ask them to help release and heal your fear of rejection (replace with your present issue).

Ask for this release through the mind grid level, the DNA level, the karmic contract level and the core soul level and beyond.

Ask for this healing from below the centre of the Earth to beyond your moment of self.

Through all the levels and bodies,

All the lifetimes including the present lifetime.

Heal all the damage from this situation.

Bring the healing into the present, now.

With that, I usually feel a weight lift off my body, a pressure somewhere or a rush of energy. Sometimes even just a knowing is a valid response. Trust what your body feels and know it is right for you. I always like to thank the Lords of Karma. Sometimes they stay if more releases are needed, or they step back.

Please modify the request to suit your needs and what resonates the best for you. Trust your intuition and inner guidance.

According to Diane Stein, the Lords of Karma are a group of spiritual beings (of high vibration) who are helping Earth, groups, and individuals be free from karmic debts.

Some of these patterns and deep core issues are so deeply embedded they may need to be peeled back in layers. This is necessary, as you deal with hurt and pain and they surface for you. You release that at a certain energy frequency and then sometimes a little later on, you face a similar issue again. However you are at a deeper level of understanding and you release it at that level. This 'peeling back the layers' does not happen with everything, however the deep issues such as fears, separation issues, trust, truth and self love can be more deeply ingrained. If this is the case for you, please persist with your releasing and feel your freedom and the 'new' each time you commit to breaking free, and before you know it you won't have an issue with that which once caused you pain.

As we lift free from the wheel of karma we move into the spiral of grace. I am here to tell you, if you don't feel or know it already, that the time of karma has come to an end. We are just clearing the old residual blocks now and we are making no new karma. However, if you believe and 'think' that there is still karma and the need for 'what goes around comes around', then you are holding yourself in karma. Open your mind, take a deep look at your thoughts and the world you are creating with them, and try thinking in new ways. When you think in new ways you bring new things into your life. As the old karmic beliefs drop away from us all and the earth too, we move beyond that space of pain and suffering and into this beautiful space of love and inner peace. You may have experienced this feeling at times or maybe often, and as we continue to lighten our energy frequency, by letting go of that which is holding us back, then you will bathe longer and longer in this beautiful space.

Consider what your beliefs are about karma and hurt and pain, and challenge those beliefs. Do your beliefs conflict with your inner knowing? Trust your knowing, it is a much higher and lighter vibration, and is more aligned with truth than the beliefs are.

Beliefs and old conditioning really control how the world is for us. I will give you an example of a client, my husband and I did an intuitive energy healing for one day. We worked hard with Malcolm (that isn't his real name for privacy purposes), going with the flow and drawing powerful energy in to help with his healing. As usual I was speaking as I worked. I find I tend to do this when we are working with mental or mind energy blocks with clients. As I was doing what I needed to do I was sharing it with him. I got to a very deep part and we released it, I could feel this energy block leaving Malcolm, however he then began to send it back into its old place. Affirming for himself that no-one can ever heal him and he will be stuck in this pain forever. Now, Malcolm's beliefs made this energy block I was removing, fling back into its old place. My husband was having the same troubles with what he was doing. A healing session with two healers that would usually take less than an hour took four hours and nothing much was set into place because he was 'willing' it back there with his beliefs.

Malcolm's story reminds us just how powerful our mind thoughts, beliefs and old conditioning are and how they create the world we live in.

If you believe that you will never be healed for whatever reason, then your belief will hold true. If you believe that you are always punished for something you did in the past, then you will bring into your life situations where you feel punished. Now, in this moment more than ever we must break down those old conditions and find the truth out for ourselves. And not have it based on what others have told us or what we believe on the news or in a text book. Wipe that slate clean and create your life based on your knowing, your truth and integrity.

The best and simplest affirmation I have found that may help you let go of old conditioning, old beliefs and to help you welcome healing and freedom into your life is this...

'I am willing to change' Louise Hay

It sounds simple, but if you repeat this to yourself as many times as you remember each day, and really put a lot of energy and focus into what you are saying, then you can watch your life change and transform. When we let go of the need to control (often we don't even realise that that is what we are doing) then we open our world up to exciting and new possibilities that are completely endless.

Self Healing Recommendation

To assist you in all areas of your life, in specific self healing and gaining control again of your life, I recommend the use of meditation and visualisation. Positive visualisation is extremely beneficial in bringing you into a stronger sense of health and balance. Anything from depression to cancer, visualisation has been proven to assist in the self healing process. The recommended time to put aside for such positive thinking is 1 to 3 times a day for 10 to 30 minutes. Before sleep and after awaking are seen as the best times. No matter what treatment you are getting from a medical professional, naturopath or energy healer, visualisation will help. It helps to utilise the treatments already being used, and helps maintain a level of health.

The strongest form of visualisation is one that sits well with you as an individual. The only thing that must be followed is that it must be a positive thought or vision. Remember if you have trouble visualising, the more you do it the clearer it will become, and always KNOW it is working and know it is there.

Make some time for yourself to be undisturbed if possible, give this nurturing time to you. Find a comfortable position for your body.

Draw a few nice deep breathes, drawing them right into your body, feeling and getting to know how your body feels and what is going on with it. Allow your body to become heavy and relaxed. When you feel ready begin your visualisation. Some ideas are: to imagine something that pours over the disease or pain, breaking it down or making it shrink, but not harming any healthy cells or imagine love pouring into the area and offering love to the pain or disease. Try and hold the vision for as long as you can. You may like to imagine the most beautiful peaceful music flowing into the area and carrying away your diseased or painful cells, and the music replaces them with love and healing. You may like to visualise a colour entering the area and filling it with love and healing. See it and know it is happening and is there. You may like to use affirmations like: "I love myself" ~ "I am happy, healthy and light" ~ "I am loved and supported."

See yourself as fully healthy, full of vitality, disease free and fulfilling your life and goals with joy.

During this time of change and bringing in these new ways, please always nurture you, and treat yourself to a nice hot bath or massage as often as you require. Speak nicely to yourself, and always BE KIND TO YOU. You ARE the most important person in your life, sing your name and love it!! Love who you are.

Chapter 11 – Spiritual Surgery

Several chapters ago you may remember me talking a little bit about spiritual surgery. In this chapter I will talk a whole lot more about it as it is a healing method that I feel very passionate about.

I will take you back to an autumn day back in May 2001. It was the day before mother's day and a few days before my 25th birthday. My spiritual friend Pat and I ventured out into the beautiful Derwent Valley, West of Hobart. We went for quite a long drive into the countryside. This was an exciting and unknown adventure for me. I hadn't done anything like this before. I had always been interested in basic 'new age' like things like astrology and palm reading, but had never done a course before. When I asked Pat (who arranged the day), what spiritual surgery was all about, she didn't know either. So we both approached our day ready to embrace whatever was taught to us.

We found this beautiful little cottage and I met Pat's friend Margaret who would be teaching us this day. Another lady arrived and the four of us connected nicely. We all sat in Margaret's sunny living room, which was a comfort on this cool day.

Firstly Margaret talked about the theory side of things. Sharing with us that, spiritual surgeons are spiritual beings who perform surgery on us, our clients, and animals. We were led through Barbara Brennan's 'Hands of Light' book and I was mesmerised by the sketches and drawings. They showed an energetic view of a spiritual surgery healing taking place. We learnt that many surgeries done in a physical surgery in hospitals could be done by the spiritual surgeons, and that these surgeons had access to amazing laser, crystal and healing tools that were yet to be used in a physical operating room.

My mind soared as I listened to what Margaret was sharing. A little later in the morning she channelled each of our spiritual surgeons, as she held my hand and breathed deeply, she wrote down the words 'crystal devas – amethyst and rose quartz.' I couldn't believe it, under my top, on a pendant I wore both of these stones. They were totally out of view. This was total confirmation for me!

After a lovely lunch it was time to learn how to 'do' spiritual surgery. Because there were three of us participating we worked on one person at a time, which meant two healers to one receiver. I called my spiritual surgeons into my aura to help me, and I felt the energy immediately. I placed my hands where I needed to. I had never done anything like this before, yet something felt so familiar about it.

I experienced a lot of sensations in my body during these healing sessions. Lots of eye flickering; my head felt heavy and tingly; hot, cold and twitching hands and feelings throughout my body.

On this day something incredible opened up for me. Pat and I left feeling so excited and uplifted and for the first time ever I drove home 'knowing' everything was safe on our journey in the car.

I was so excited and practiced immediately when I got home on my sister Louise, she also experienced eye flickering. This was so fun. That night I dreamed wonderful dreams about crystals and my amazing day. I woke up feeling a sense of peace and a different, kind of new knowledge. My intuition suddenly 'kicked in' and I had all these urges, feelings and knowing, and everything was perfect.

The day after the Spiritual Surgery course was mother's day. Louise and I decided to take my kids to visit our mother who lived about two hours drive away. Due to my parents separating when we were a young age, and my sisters and I living with our father, we didn't get to spend many mother's days with our mother, so we were all excited about this.

Whilst at mum's I was excited to share all I had learned the day before at the spiritual surgery practitioner's course. I did some healing on one of my other sisters, Caroline and also on mum.

As I was doing mum's healing she felt a little 'pop' in her nose. It was in this spot that mum had a cyst, and she hadn't been able to breathe properly from her nose for four years. After the 'pop' her nose cleared and she could breathe through it again. We were both very excited about this. I felt there was more work to be done on mum, but we were running out of time that day, so I mentioned I would send her some healing via distance.

At this time I didn't really know how or what to do with healing via distance, but I felt the words come out from my mouth very strongly, so who was I to argue?

Later that evening after all had settled. My ex husband and I decided to watch a movie on our new television. With the movie preparing to start a bright green light splashed across one of the corners of the television screen. Much to my ex's disgust it remained even when the television was turned 'off.' For quite a while the green section stayed. As I stood watching this strange light, out of the corner of my eyes I saw lights flashing around the mattress on the floor. I mentioned them to my ex but he couldn't see them, and after he grew frustrated with the coloured corner on the television screen he decided that no movie would be watched by him tonight!

I continued to stand, mesmerised by these flashing lights, which continued to get stronger. I would describe these like flashing fluorescent lights flicking all around the mattresses edge. After ten minutes I got the message and feeling that it was time to send my mother distant spiritual surgery. With that intention, the green light on the television disappeared!

I laid on the mattress to send some distant spiritual surgery. I worked with some crystals and felt a very strong 'lightness' flow over my body. As I relaxed further my body felt like it lifted from the mattress and began to pivot from a point near my navel. I felt my whole being pivot and spin from side to side around that centre point. I sent healing to mum and a few others.

For the coming few years I did a fair bit of spiritual surgery on others and myself. It was a couple of years later that I was introduced to a new spiritual surgeon working with me.

I had been participating in a local shamanic meditation circle for about a year, when this one evening we were asked to all lay down and to try a different position to meditate in. As I was used to doing it in a comfortable chair sitting up, I felt lying down was a distraction. I found it hard to follow what Cheryl, our meditation facilitator was saying. So I decided that I would just do my own thing. So in my mind I went to a meditation space I like to visit, which I call my 'meditation room.' Here I was greeted by a short man, and I felt an instant buzzing in my left ear. I was told that his name was Dr Raymond and that he is my new spiritual surgeon. He also told me that when he needed to work with me on clients that he would buzz in my left ear.

This taught me a lot. I learnt that it is good to break habits, because they can be limiting our truest potential as well as Divine messages. For if I had meditated in the same position that evening like I usually did, then my journey would no doubt have been a lot different. Changing habits create new experiences!

I worked with Dr Raymond for some time and here I will share with you some spiritual surgeries that have happened for clients I have worked with:

When a friend of mine had a strange lump at the top of his foot that was full of 'fluid' I asked for permission from him to do some spiritual surgery. He agreed I got to work. I called Dr Raymond forward and in my mind I saw what was happening. With my hands on my friend's foot, I saw Dr Raymond's spiritual hands sort of gently working through mine and into my friend's foot. In my mind I saw him make an incision at the bottom of the foot, where he then began to 'pull out' a red ball of energy. This ball of energy looked like red string wound around itself to form a ball of red string. This energy ball was quite large. Once it was removed by my surgeon, he sealed the cut area with laser light and rubbed some of his 'magic healing cream' onto the area. My friends foot, which had been troubling him for many days healed quickly, but not before a massive bruise appeared. This bruise moved through the usual bruise colours at an accelerated rate.

Before I share more, I wanted to talk to you more about my spiritual surgeon, Dr Raymond. He worked with me for around 9 years and I recall after he buzzed in my left ear, I would see a vision of him carrying his 'bag of tricks' - this is what I called it. It was a black leathery looking bag which held everything in it. Often during surgeries he would finish by rubbing his 'white magic healing cream' onto the area he worked. He told me that this healing cream would speed up the healing process, especially for the physical aspect of the healing. Another time I recall during a surgery, Dr Raymond handed me a pair of his special 'glasses' and when I energetically put them on, I saw amazing things in the body. I was seeing things through his eyes. It was so incredible.

Another time I sent some distant healing to a man who had sliced the tops of his fingers off during a work accident. You may imagine the pain this might cause. One evening I sent distant spiritual surgery to him, and in my mind's eye I saw his hand pointing down with what looked like liquid bones dripping from the ends. I was told by Dr Raymond that this was helping repair the ends of his fingers along with the damaged nerves. After this the pain began to lessen for him.

I have taught spiritual surgery practitioner's course several times now and it is growing in popularity. In March 2010 during the course I was teaching in Sydney I felt my surgeon begin to change, and I no longer felt Dr Raymond around. A few weeks later my new surgeon Amealia was channelled through to work with me. Her energy is completely different to Dr Raymond, and she quickly began working personally with me. Amealia resonates strongly with crystals and one day whilst I had some self healing time with my husband's smoky quartz crystal, I was pretty much knocked out. It was like I was under some sort of anaesthetic. I felt so much energy and activity around my feet, legs and hips. I was sort of aware but at the same time not. Like I was at that stage of 'in between' sleep. One thing I recall strongly is that I couldn't move my body, I felt paralysed and meanwhile my body jolted a lot and even a few times I felt some pain, but I knew it was for a good cause and I trust my spiritual guides. I drew a picture of Amealia which you can enjoy in my healing energy cards (currently available) or my oracle cards (released 2011).

At a Spiritual Surgery Course in the morning we talk about the theory side of things and I also channel through everyone's spiritual surgeon. In the afternoon we switch into practical, now this phase I just love. We usually have a mix of people, for some this is their very first spiritual course and for others they are looking at adding this tool to their healing toolbox. In any case I love seeing the participants get so into this time. Usually I quietly connect with each pair and draw their auras and energy how I see it whilst the healing is taking place. Often there is confirmation in it about what they felt or saw themselves. By the end of the day most people are buzzing with energy and excitement for what happened to them while they received or channelled the healing energies.

Spiritual surgery is non invasive. It doesn't involve any blood or physical manipulation. It all happens totally on a spiritual level, but works into every area of our being - the physical, emotional, mental and spiritual levels. Spiritual surgery is extremely empowering, allowing you to flow with your intuition and really open up to your surgeon working through you. This healing, like all others I do is not energy draining. In fact, in my opinion if you are doing any form of healing or service correctly then you shouldn't feel drained but uplifted with energy. If you are feeling exhausted after you have given a healing session then it is important to make sure that you are not giving away your own energy. This is usually the case when we work with someone we know and love, especially our children. When working with those we care about we can often give so much of our own energy, leaving us feeling drained.

When you are *flowing* with your healing or surgery you will open your being up and allow the energy to flow through you. It flows through you 'charging you' as it travels. Make sure you are feeling charged after giving a healing and if not, ask your body why.

It's also important to bear in mind that if you have done a lot of healing sessions in one day, maybe at an expo or fair, then you may certainly feel tired. It is just like any other day of work and service. It's when you feel drained after one or two sessions that suggests exploring it further so you don't exhaust yourself totally.

> *Exercise (v): Spiritual surgery distant healing for you now...*
>
> *This is for you if you would like to receive some spiritual surgery right now via distance. If you choose not to, then please overlook this exercise.*
>
> *If you have any of my card decks which contain my spiritual surgeon Amealia in it, then please collect it and place her card face down on your body somewhere or place her nearby.*

Become aware of your breathing... feel your breath slow and deepen, don't strain but flow with your natural rhythm.

Allow your gaze on these words to soften and really begin to feel and come into tune with your body in this moment.

How is your body feeling? How are you feeling emotionally or mentally? Don't judge what you see or feel, just acknowledge it.

Spiritual surgeons know exactly what you need in this moment, so please open up your energy and trust them. Try not to block their work by thinking you should have this or that, allow them to flow their magic into you. Surrender and allow...

I send you now my Spiritual Surgeon Amealia, she stands behind you and places her hands gently on your crown chakra. Your crown chakra is at the top of your head. This is your chakra that connects you with the world beyond the physical. You may feel a bit of tingling or other sensations up there, allow yourself to feel...

We ask Amealia to perform the surgery in the best way that your higher self, your spiritual helpers, and she see fit. We know that they will do what is necessary for your highest good in this moment.

Allow Amealia and the surgery team to work on you for as long as you need.

You may even find it continues into the night or over a few days. Trust and flow.

When Amealia's work is complete she will give you an energy gift and then step out of your space.

Breathe now and feel... please return to this section anytime you feel you would like to receive some spiritual surgery. Each time you may feel something different. And it doesn't matter where Amealia works the energy will go where it is needed.

If anything stirred up for you physically, emotionally or mentally please know this is part of your healing. I recommend that you drink lots of water to help cleanse the energy that may have come to the surface, listen to your body – if it wants to rest, eat light meals etc, please honour this and always be kind and gentle with yourself. So please don't be hard on you, think and feel loving thoughts towards yourself.

Chapter 12 – Chakras

Chakras are energy centres that draw in life force. There are many different layers of the aura, and each layer resides on a slightly higher frequency than the layer before it. Each different layer contains a different set of chakras. The most commonly known, which we will also talk about here are the seven major chakras which reside in the first layer of the aura, the etheric body.

We have talked a lot about chakras previously and will continue to do so. For me, the chakras are keys to help me understand what is happening in certain areas of the body. Building a sound knowledge of these chakras also helps me understand more about the colours and their meaning. This is because each chakra's energy vibration is in tune or alignment with one of the colours of the rainbow. As the energy frequency changes the colour and the sound changes too. Just like moving up or down on the keys on a piano. The same applies with colour.

This chapter will be fairly in depth because to me this knowledge is important. It will help you understand more about what is going on in your body and maybe why that part aches or why you continually hurt on that side and so on.

As I move through each chakra and its meaning, I have also created this exercise for you to do as we go. To help you really feel and connect with that centre. As you read the words I also ask that you feel and connect with that area of your body. Pay attention to any strange sensations, visions, thoughts or interruptions that seem to occur in that moment. If you would like to work with some crystals or Healing Energy Cards please have those handy. This will be fairly long, so I suggest you allow some time for this section of powerful healing and the sharing of knowledge about the seven major chakras.

Exercise (vi): Connecting with your chakras

Bring your focus gently to your breathing and when you are ready, soften your focus on these words and begin to become more sensitive to your body in the here and now.

*We are going to start by focusing on your **base chakra**. Your base chakra is at the base of your spine. This is your first chakra of the major seven. The colour that resonates with this centre is red.*

Your base chakra is positioned at the base of your spine. On an energy level this centre is your most physical chakra and helps you stay nice and grounded and present in this moment. Your base chakra represents your physical entity.

Take a few moments now to connect with your base chakra at the base of your spine. You may sense it gently spinning or you may not feel much at all for now. Expand your feeling, let go of any doubts or blocks happening in your thinking and allow yourself to feel. Take your time and really connect with this centre.

How does this area feel? Have you been experiencing physical pain or discomfort around here lately? How does the rest of your body feel as you connect with your base chakra? Try not to be judgmental, simply feel instead.

Gently imagine this area filling and expanding with red light. Feel any pain or discomfort held here wash away. Take your time bathing in this red energy.

When you are ready gently draw your focus up from your base chakra to your sacral chakra.

*Your **sacral chakra** sits just below your navel and is in line with your spleen. At your spleen* *macrophages are manufactured to cleanse your blood and boost your immune system.*

Begin to really feel this centre, you may even like to place a crystal or your hand on there to help you heal and release any old energy you hold within your sacral chakra.

Your sacral chakra is your centre for emotional, sexual and creative energies. It is usually orange in colour and often those people who are sensitive to energy, who are called clairsentient, can be quite sensitive in this area.

How does your sacral chakra feel right now? How are your emotions? Have you been feeling blocked with creativity lately? Get in tune with your sacral chakra and this entire area, including your lower back.

These major chakras have a front and back aspect. And they draw in energy from both sides. The only exception to this is the base and crown chakras who are opposites of each other.

When you are ready imagine this area of your body filling with bright orange light. This orange light clears any old emotions stored in here, which includes suppression of feeling and any blocks in acknowledging your feminine side.

Whether we have physically manifested as a male or female in this lifetime, we all have feminine and masculine aspects. And this sacral chakra is aligned with those feminine qualities.

Hold your focus on the orange light for as long as you need to.

When you are ready gently draw your focus up to your next chakra which is your solar plexus.

*Your **solar plexus chakra** is your power centre. It is your centre for personal power, strength and courage. It usually vibrates at the colour yellow and is the balance of our previously discussed chakra, being that it is our masculine centre.*

The solar plexus chakra is in line with your adrenals and this gland produces hydrocortisone which helps regulate the way your body uses food and how it adjusts to stress.

If you want to, you can place a crystal or your hand onto your solar plexus – just above your navel. Become nice and sensitive to it and allow yourself to feel. Pay attention to any thoughts, feelings or visions that surface for you in this moment. They are all connected and are clues in helping you understand what may be out of balance in your life.

Breathe in the power of your breath through this area. Breathe the life force and the colour yellow into your solar plexus chakra. Allow the yellow light to wash away any feelings of powerlessness, any lack of courage or inner strength. Imagine your solar plexus like a golden sun in your belly. This golden sun radiates energy, light and strength (also out the back of you too), warming and soothing any pain or discomfort.

Bathe in the yellow light for as long as you need to right now. Feel your lower three centres aligning and coming into perfect balance. (Your base chakra, connecting with your physical being; your sacral chakra connecting with your emotional being and your solar plexus connecting with your mental being.) You come into perfect alignment in the here and now.

You may even like to run these energies together by using your imagination and visualisation;

imagine the colours blending together as you breathe up and down, focusing on those lower three chakras. Take your time. If you find your mind thoughts get in the way, try giving your mind thoughts no thought, thus no energy. When you don't focus on them they will melt into the background. The more you focus on them, even if you are thinking that you 'shouldn't be thinking that now, you should be relaxing' - the stronger those thoughts become. Allow them to flow in and out at the background of your mind.

On your next breath in, draw your attention up to your fourth chakra, your heart. Your **heart chakra** *is in alignment with your thymus gland, which produces 'T' cells for the immune system and to protect against foreign matters. Your heart chakra is usually green, however can also be pink, this is your centre for love of self, others and all creation. Your heart chakra is the centre of your system, the bridge between the lower and upper three chakras.*

Imagine this area of your body filling up with green or pink light. Trust what comes through first, sometimes you may have a mix of both colours - nothing you are seeing or feeling is wrong, so please trust your intuition. Feel and know this light is penetrating deeply within your heart as it calls forward any old love hurts or scars, any attacks towards self (like putting yourself down, being judgmental or not accepting yourself). Allow this green or pink light to wash those wounds away, clearing your heart and bringing it back to life. As that old energy leaves, feel the colours intensify as more love fills your heart.

Your heart chakra also includes that back aspect, which is your upper back, and everything within this area of your body. Breathe this beautiful green or pink light deeply into your lungs and heart, and feel this love being distributed via your blood cells and the oxygen, going to every corner of your body. Feel it swirl and settle into its rightful place.

Allowing your heart centre to heal and balance will assist you on many levels throughout your being and with your life. As you surrender any old heart pain and become more conscious in the choices you make, to live from your heart, your life will transform. When we choose to move our focus from our ego or lower mind and into our heart and intuition, something magical happens - we move out of fear and worry and into love and harmony. How beautiful is this? This is the place where true miracles occur.

As your heart chakra expands with love, bring your focus and attention up to your fifth chakra, your throat. This is the first chakra in those upper three and therefore is your first more 'spiritual' or higher vibrating centre.

Your **throat chakra** *is usually the colour blue and is your centre for expression, communication and truth. On your physical body, it is in alignment with your thyroid gland. The thyroid produces thyroxin which converts oxygen and food into useable energy.*

The throat chakra can be quite sensitive. Sometimes as people are speaking, sharing or even talking about the throat centre, as we are now, some tickling or coughing may occur. So please take note and feel how your throat is right now. Do you suddenly have a tickle there? Has your breathing changed or do you hear a strange sound? All hearing is also connected to your throat chakra; the ability to talk less and listen more is governed by this centre.

Breathe and really focus on your throat centre. If you want to you can move a crystal up to this area or place your hand gently there. How is it feeling? Be open to feeling and try not to be too judgmental, just observe. You are not doing this to be hard or critical to yourself, but to be aware and learn how to step outside your drama or pain and see it from a different perspective, looking for insight and the lessons - to see the bigger picture.

As you focus on your throat chakra imagine a beautiful blue light entering there to heal and balance your throat centre at this time. Allow the perfect shade to come forward into your consciousness, if you have trouble seeing it, please know it is there weaving its magic through you. Feel the blue light swirl and carry away any blocks that are being held in your throat centre. Feel them leave your body for good. That old energy is replaced with love and truth. Feel the love in the form of this blue light flow all around your neck now. If there are any tensions there allow this light to soften and relax those muscles.

The energy shifts a little as you gently draw your focus up to your sixth centre, your **third eye chakra***. As I sit here bringing this through for this healing, my attention was drawn for a moment to the tree outside my window. I saw a large raven plonk itself down on one of the tree branches, after a little observing I saw a swarm of smaller birds dive down and try to attack this much larger raven. The squawking from the smaller birds suggests that the raven is close to the nest carrying their young on this spring day on the South-East coast of Tasmania. The drama has ended now, however I felt there was an important connection in this moment to the third eye chakra that I had just switched to when the bird drama unfolded.*

This reminds me about the predator / prey energy reflected in many areas of our world. Not only with animals preying on smaller animals for food. But also, relationships like; the giver and the receiver, the victim and the perpetrator etc. It sure gives us something to think about and feel in our bodies. Everyone has an opinion, however I try my hardest to not see either predator or prey as good or bad, but as different perspectives. Have we deferred from the current focus of our third eye chakra? I feel not, this all reminds us about the balance.

Your third eye chakra is on your forehead between your eyes. As we focus here you may feel a bit of tingling or a strange sensation in the area. If you are lying down and are able to, you may like to place a small crystal on your third eye chakra, or maybe your hand if you want to.

Your third eye chakra is where a lot of information comes in for you, divine information, old and ancient information from the past and the awakening of old memories. This is your centre for intuition, vision and trust. You may not read anywhere else where the word trust is connected to the third eye chakra, however through my healing experience I know that we can be the most intuitive person in the world, but if we don't trust what we sense then our intuition is just like air, we can't do much with it in our lives. So trust is very important in this area. A lot of people who have trust issues may also have blocks in this third eye chakra. Your third eye chakra is usually an indigo colour, a mix of blue and violet.

As we connect with the third eye chakra become sensitive to yours and how it feels right now. Does it feel slightly heavy, pressured or tingly? Using your breathing again, relax your body and breathe out any old energy or blocks you are holding within this area. These may be trust issues, blocks in your psychic senses, vision or anything else. Sometimes we are told or get a feeling what the block is and other times we don't need to know. All you need to do is be willing to surrender and let go of everything that is holding you back in the here and now.

As you do this, imagine an indigo light flowing into your third eye chakra, feel or know it entering and it begins to swirl there. This light, along with the others we have focused on has two purposes, to help you release and to anchor love and light into the area. Usually it is best to release the old first, as this makes room for the new. It's like when we have a shower to clean our physical body; our body cannot be clean and new until the dirt is removed.

Allow the indigo light to carry away all your hurt and pain, blocks and old energy from your third eye chakra. Surrender it all, let it go now, it is safe for you to do this. You can use the light and your out breath to help you release at the same to if you want to. Experiment and find a way to release that works for you.

When you are ready the indigo light slightly switches its intention, and begins to add bright, fresh and loving energy into your third eye chakra. Every 'in' breath you take intensifies this light. Allow it to grow and open this chakra. Feel the indigo light flowing around your whole head, lightening up your mind energy and mind thoughts, and freeing you in this area. Please stay here for as long as you need to.

The energy shifts a little as you bring your focus to your **crown chakra***. This is your seventh chakra in this system. This centre is usually violet, however can also be gold, white, rainbow or silver.*

The crown chakra helps us connect with the world beyond the physical. To bridge the illusions of separation, and to experience Oneness in our lives. The crown chakra teaches us to move beyond separation and feeling different, disconnected and alone. The merging of dark / light and day / night and all other opposites into One.

As we focus on your crown chakra, you may feel some tingling up there on the top of your head or you may not feel anything, in either case you will experience what is unique for you in this moment. If you want to place your hand on your head for a little while please do, this will be helpful for your self-healing, especially if you are releasing separation, loneliness or disconnection blocks.

Imagine a colour entering your crown chakra. This may be a violet, white, gold, rainbow or silver light, allow your self to trust your first impressions. Again if you have trouble seeing or feeling this, please know it is there, don't doubt, but trust. Allow this light to cleanse your crown chakra, pulling away all blocks, barriers and issues stuck in there that may be holding you back from fully living, loving and experiencing life. Surrender and let go, give your self permission to be free. Take your time, take all the time you require.

When you are ready allow the light here to switch a little and feel love, oneness and light fill your crown chakra now, feel your crown, (including your brain) come to life with light. Feel your connection, open up to visions and messages and know that you do belong somewhere, you belong here. If you weren't meant to be here, you wouldn't be here!

When you are ready feel the light from your crown chakra expand and flow down your spine and into the rest of your body, aligning all the chakras together, in one connection. Feel how balanced, grounded and centred you are right now.

You can refer to this section anytime you feel you would like to experience some deep healing and cleansing. Each time you travel back here you may find that your experience is different. Trust the flow and the uniqueness of you and the moment. You may need to sit with this energy for a few days, trust how your body feels.

As you open up more to your chakras you may notice changes flow into every area of your life. As you heal, let go and release from the old and anchor the new and true into your body, you raise your vibration, not only of your aura, but also your chakras. It is very exciting.

I work with chakras a lot in my healing work, even when I am teaching, I can feel the collective energy of the group in my chakras and body, this helps me know what to focus on as I trust my intuition.

Chakra Summary

1. BASE chakra.

Colour: Red

Location: At the base of your spine.

Brief Description: Your chakra for grounding and survival instincts.

2. SACRAL chakra.

Colour: Orange

Location: Just below your navel.

Brief Description: Your chakra for emotional, sexual and creative energies. Your feminine centre.

3. SOLAR PLEXUS chakra.

Colour: Yellow

Location: Just above your navel.

Brief Description: Your chakra for personal power, strength and courage. Your masculine centre.

4. HEART chakra.

Colour: Green / Pink

Location: Over your physical heart.

Brief Description: Your chakra for love of self, others and all creation. The centre of your Being.

5. THROAT chakra.

Colour: Blue

Location: In the centre of your neck, at the front.

Brief Description: Your chakra for expression, communication and truth.

6. THIRD EYE chakra.

Colour: Indigo

Location: On your forehead, between your eye brows.

Brief Description: Your chakra for vision, intuition and trust.

7. CROWN chakra.

Colour: Purple / gold / white / silver

Location: At the crown of your head.

Brief Description: Your chakra that helps you connect with the world beyond the physical.

Chapter 13 – Crystal Healing

Wonderful tools to help you heal and activate your chakras are crystals. Crystals are simply amazing tools shared from the earth. These days you must be careful and make sure yours is a natural piece, as there are many manmade stones coming out of places like Asia, which are flooding the internet market. If the stone is flawless, then it is most likely 'lab-made.'

When I was a healing priestess during that past life in Atlantis I worked a lot with healing crystals. In fact during those ancient days crystals where used to generate power and to time travel - among many other things. Crystals are used today in our computers and technologies.

Every word I have shared with you here has been accompanied by my clear quartz crystal. I use crystals every day in my healing work and personal life.

In those ancient days of Atlantis I had a friend who lived in the mountains, he was a hermit and would find me the most amazing and sacred healing stones to use in my healing temple. This friend came back into my life as a female early on in the forming of Temple of Balance and she was still finding me amazing crystals and stones! In fact the one I have with me in this moment is a seed crystal. She found and sent it to me from the other side of the world. I love how this works. How we meet people and experience things in the right moment, and many times it has such an ancient connection, it makes it all even more perfect.

Crystals can weave their magic and help you with any situation whether it is physical, emotional, mental or spiritual. Every stone has its own unique qualities which can help you. Crystals have auras, and this energy has the ability to give to you certain qualities it contains, and also to draw out of you certain energy blocks that you no longer require in your life.

Crystals also resonate with the chakra frequencies. So knowing that blue is the colour for the throat chakra, if you feel blocked in the throat or have a sore throat then a blue crystal may help with that.

The ancient blue and gold coloured stone of Lapis lazuli helps with motion sickness, headaches, opening your third eye chakra, protecting your immune system and working on your throat chakra.

One of my favourite crystals to sleep with for a great night's sleep and to help me dream helpful things is red jasper. This stone is so nurturing and is also known as the 'shaman's stone' which is very helpful to hold during shamanic meditation journeys. Because it is a red brown colour it also resonates with our base chakra, thus, keeping us grounded in the here and now.

Crystals come in all shapes and sizes. Some naturally shaped in points, wands, clusters or rocks. And others polished and carved. I personally work with all sorts and types. Depending on what I am drawn to in any moment.

A generator crystal is the way it has been polished. It is usually thicker at the base and thinner at the top, forming a tapered tower. As I can see and feel energy I see a lot of concentrated energy at the base of the generator, and this spins slightly longer and longer as it comes to the point and then extends out from the point. This is a great stone shape for charging a room during meditation or a spiritual gathering. I also like to place mine with the base resting on my chakras to pull old energy out. It tends to draw old energy up from within our bodies, as if the generator is a magnet. I also like to do the opposite sometimes, and place the pointed end on my chakra or skin, and allow the high energy vibrations from the crystal's energy to draw down Universal energy for healing, meditation or channelling.

My 'seed' crystal is seeded with ancient memories and information from ancient times. I know I had this 'seed' crystal's sister during my Atlantean lives. The 'seed' crystals are naturally formed points of clear quartz. Intermittent lines and scratchings that look like a barcode have formed on the sides of these stones. Within the crystal are amazing energies and memories to call upon and work with. And rubbing your thumb or fingers along this 'barcode' can bring a lot of information and energy from the crystal into your being. Often this can bring forward a high pitched ring in one ear. This is an indication that you are 'downloading' important information, just like a computer downloading its information. The ringing when broken down into a slower speed is like codes. They are being embedded into your being as a seed, waiting for the perfect moment, energy and space to begin to sprout and come to life. You are remembering.

Another fascinating stone which I love right now is called a Shree Yantra. A Shree Yantra is from India and when I first saw one of these I couldn't believe it, because for many years I have been doing activation healings, where ancient multidimensional symbols and codes are embedded into my clients crown chakra. These symbols and codes have been made by my fingers and hands. The best way I could ever describe these symbols and codes was like a 'multidimensional mandala.' And when I recently saw a Shree Yantra made of pure clear quartz, I looked at it from the base perspective and it is in fact a mandala. The Shree Yantra is like a little tower or temple, it has perfectly carved levels and layers, and when looking at it from above or below, it does resemble a mandala. I love working with mine during healing sessions, but also for my self healing. I place it on my third eye chakra. I have done this with many crystals during the past decade and I know how powerful it can be. With the Shree Yantra I didn't feel a lot at the start, then I felt the energy coming down in layers, the energy began to intensify, before long it began to pulsate bursts of energy into my third eye and it spread around my body. This is an amazing stone.

If you are struggling from grief due to loss, then the gentle orange carnelian is very helpful for this. Carnelian helps balance our emotions and also helps us adjust to change.

Many crystals require cleansing to rid them of the old stored energy they have gathered from helping you / others, or just from 'sitting around.' Depending on what you are going through and how often you are using the crystal determines how often you cleanse it. You may feel that your crystal feels 'heavy' or 'tacky'; this is an indication that cleansing may be a great idea.

There are many ways to cleanse your stones. I will share a few ideas with you here.

Exercise (vii): Cleansing Your crystal

a) *Hold your stone under running water, like a tap and imagine all the impurities leaving it via the water.*

b) *Hold your stone over sacred smoke, like a fire, smudge stick, incense or candle (being cautious not to burn yourself). Imagine the smoke carrying the impurities away.*

c) *Place your stone in salt water overnight or for a couple of days in the presence of the moon / sun. A full moon is a great time for this.*

d) *Find somewhere on dirt to place your stone for cleansing and imagine that old energy leaving and being drawn into the earth for cleansing and transformation.*

e) *Other crystals can be used to cleanse your crystal. Clusters (a group of smaller crystals on one base) are good. And some stones like citrine never require cleansing. So citrine is a great cluster to use for cleansing other stones.*

> *You do this by placing your crystal that requires cleansing onto the cluster. Imagining all impurities leaving it.*
>
> *f)* *Using your intentions as you hold your crystal in your hand will also work. Imagine a coloured light, white is a good one, to flow over your stone carrying with it all the impurities.*

Please note that some crystals do not like water, so please make sure yours is a 'harder stone' before placing it in water. Some softer ones can dissolve in water. Soft ones that shouldn't go in water are selenite, calcite, amazonite, kyanite and lepidolite. With those you can use sacred smoke or your intentions.

After my stone is cleansed, I like to then 'charge' it with energy. My favourite way to do this is by working with the sun. I imagine the sun's rays charging and bringing my crystal to life again. All I do is place my individual or group of crystals in the sun and I know they are being charged or filled with nice and new energy.

I always keep at least one stone on me at all times. I have a crystal pouch, where I keep a few of my smaller stones with me. In my pouch you may find some clear quartz, citrine, black tourmaline, Shree Yantra, seed crystal, apophyllite or blue lace agate. I would also add any tumble stone that I felt particularly drawn to in the moment.

Have you heard others say that they don't want you touching their crystals? To me this is an old energy approach that is not necessary in these times. Because the power of our mind is creating our world more than ever before, if we believe that others will 'spread negative energy' to our stones when touching, then that belief manifests and becomes your reality. If you know that nothing can penetrate or leave negative energies attached to it, then nothing can affect your crystal. Consider what you believe, what you have been told by others and what you know to be the truth. I always follow the latter. So I share my crystals and have no problem with anyone holding or using them.

Here I am sharing with you all of this information about crystals but how do you actually 'use' them? Firstly know that you can't do anything wrong with them. They cannot harm you (unless you have a belief that tells you otherwise). They come in all shapes and sizes, so let me break their shapes down a bit for you;

> **Tumble stones** – these are very common and only cost a little bit usually. These are great to place in your pocket, your wallet, your crystal pouch, to hold in your hand, place on your body for self healing, and to place under your pillow to help you sleep.

> **Clusters** – these are usually on a natural base (a part of the actual crystal) and on the surface are tiny or sometimes larger individual points, but there are lots of them. Clusters are great for room clearing. When you place one in a room, office, studio etc it will inject its energy into the environment. These are great for people who work in an office and feel attacked or uncomfortable there. A cluster will help boost the energy of these surroundings.

> **Spheres and eggs** – these are among my favourite right now. They are wonderful to hold. Depending on the size you may be able to place them in your pocket. I sleep with mine in my hand, and if it is a big one I store it under my arm. Spheres and eggs are great to gently massage yourself, especially the temples, face and eyes if you have a headache. They can also be good to place on a stand in a room or on your bedside, healing, or reading table.

Points, generators and wands – depending on the size you can probably put this in your pocket. If it is a small one in the form of a pendant, they are great to have hanging around your neck, working on your throat / heart areas. Some wands have a rounded end, and in this case they are great for massage. Some are pointed or double pointed and these are good for running energy, especially up or down the spine, or releasing old energy.

The thing to remember with crystals is that for them to weave their most wonderful benefits to you, it is best that you have them on or as close to your person as much as possible. When you do this they are in your auric field and can do what they need to do to help you.

You can program your crystals to help with certain things. For example, if in the middle of the night my children are having a bad dream, I will offer them a crystal, as I offer it to them in my mind I ask the crystal to help them sleep. If they take it, it always works, they seem to know this and most of the time do take it when it is offered. I never force this onto my children or to others. I am at peace with what I do, I do not need to prove it to anyone, and I also have no expectations about it being wanted. So whatever theirs or others choices are I am more than accepting of.

How do you know which crystal you require? If you are in a shop and have an array of stones laid out in front of you and do not know which one or what to get, what do you do? Sometimes you may be drawn to a crystal because by its qualities (which are sometimes written near the stone – if not, ask the shop keeper as they should have a reference book or something handy) and if this is the case, trust it. Sometimes you may be drawn to the crystal by its colour or texture. Sometimes you will just know this is one you need right now.

Now let's say that you have worked out that you like and are drawn to the properties and colour of 'rose quartz' right now, you are looking at a huge group of just that one particular stone, how do you pick one of them? For me, I like to listen to my body, sometimes my eyes guide me to the one I need, because of its shape or colour. Other times I will still not completely know. In this case and if I am able to, I will pick up one at a time and will feel how they feel in my hand. Sometimes there may be an intense heat, coolness or tingling. And this will be confirmation for me that it is the right one.

Our body and entire being resonates with the crystal that we need in that moment. You may use it for many years, you may only need it for a week or two or maybe on and off over time. Sometimes we dream of crystals or see one and we just know we need it.

At times you may misplace or lose a crystal. I never worry about this, firstly because I feel it is a waste of energy to worry and secondly because I know I no longer require the benefits of that crystal, and either it needed to be returned to the Earth or will fall into the hands of someone else who needs it. Crystals have a way of finding their owners. Don't think it is any accident if you 'happen' to find a crystal somewhere.

Many years ago I went to the beach to meditate, I do this often but on this particular day it was a full moon and I love connecting with the energies of the moon. I had a small clear quartz point with me, and it wasn't until I returned home that I realised I left it at the beach in the evening darkness. I was slightly upset as I liked that stone. At the time I was learning a lot about synchronicity, so I let it go, knowing that it would fall into the right hands or stay with the Earth. You must understand my surprise when exactly two weeks later on the new moon a friend walked up to me and presented a crystal he had found at the beach and he thought I would like it. It was my crystal returned to me! I love the way the Universe works.

Crystals are very powerful tools for self healing. Most people when starting to work with them are drawn to more common and gentle stones like amethyst or rose quartz. As you get more comfortable with their energy then you can enjoy very powerful experiences, meditations and assistance from your crystals.

Chapter 14 – Healing Energy Cards

I am often asked by people 'how can you take on so many projects especially with a young family?' I find that it sort of comes naturally to me. I feel that the past five years or so have helped swing me into this space I am in now. Balance is extremely important, as well as time management. I am lucky enough to be able to spend every day working on my passions and dreams with Temple of Balance. I am a highly motivated person and my spiritual teachers just love seeding me with me ideas and inspirations, because I am so easily uplifted by them. I am not a procrastinator at all, but an 'action' Goddess. I act on my 'intuitive impulses.'

Each day is ultimately in alliance with my body. If I feel tired or unmotivated, then I will always listen to and honour my body above everything else. If I need to take some time out from my computer, I will turn it off and relax. I keep reminders every day about tasks or parts of projects I want to spend some time working on. If my body is having one of those 'rest' days, I don't argue or judge it, I just reschedule my tasks.

My days at the moment are consisting of many things. For example, I have cut my distant and phone healings / readings down to one day every other week. This gives me time to get other projects done. In the morning I spend about 30 – 60 minutes on marketing. I may then do two hours drawing, either working on current drawing orders from individuals, my own work or some projects I am doing with others. I may then book the next two hours to write some more of this book, or to do some website work or reply to emails. Depending on what I have going each day, I attempt to do a bit of each project most days if possible.

It has also been important for me to learn the word 'no!' Being a compassionate and caring person it was once easier for me to be nice and just do what others wanted, no matter what it was. However these days, with my time being more and more precious, I have to say 'no.' I always try to say it in a nice way, and am always honest with my reason why I can't do something. No matter what happens, I must always stay true to me.

Quite a few years ago I felt a strong internal knowing that I would create my own set of cards. In 2007 I discovered something extraordinary. I found out that art, colour and pattern can potentially heal the body, mind and emotions. I found out that people see their own reflections in these things. For example a strange shaped tree may look like a dragon shape to someone, but a butterfly to another. But it went deeper than this; people were feeling things through my art. See chapter 9 – Healing with colour for more information.

At this time of Temple of Balance's creation I was extremely busy working with people via distance. Doing up to six healings a day, five days a week, day and night. I needed to find something that would help these people, so they didn't have to rely on others to help them. I began to collect my healing art and draw new ones. Some came to me in a dream or vision, and other drawings just came through when I had pencil to paper. In all cases they are unique and contain so much healing energy.

When I had completed the first 32 cards and before I had them professionally printed, I carried a 6 x 4 inch printed sample of them all around with me. I would show people and observe what reflections the drawings or words had to them. One card in particular, 17. Time Tunnels would stir all kinds of reactions. Not many people 'liked' that card, it felt strange to them. When I asked them how they would feel looking into the past for their self healing, many claimed that they wouldn't 'go there.' And for me, this was another sign that these drawings, as cards, would help many.

When someone reacts to a drawing in any way, whether it is in a positive or negative way suggests that there is something they can gain in the form of healing from the cards, especially ones that are rejected. I urge people to explore any they seem to react to like that. There is great opportunity to heal within the cards.

So in November 2007 with my self-printed little pack under my arm, my friend and I went to Doreen Virtue's Angel Intuitive workshop in Northern Australia. It may seem funny, but my reason for going was to get my cards out there, at the time hoping to have Hay House pick them up for publishing, naturally any budding author's dream! I also wanted to learn about running and delivering workshops. I learnt a lot about both. In regards to my cards, I showed quite a few people I met there and they were very excited about them. I also managed to show the director of Hay House Australia, he was very nice and gave me tips to self print. He informed me that a publishing company would not look at them until I sold a lot and proved there was a real market for them.

Excited about this, I left the weekend with some tools and the feeling of being ready to take action and finally get my cards printed and out to people who need them. Strange as it was, on the plane trip home I misplaced the pre-printed pack. They vanished! At first I was a little upset, but then I noticed that the Universe was putting a fire under my backside and was telling me that these cards are needed and to get them out to people as soon as possible!

I looked into some local printing businesses and found one. With money saved I got my first five hundred packs printed. People, especially my clients began to work with them, and I would often hear them saying how wonderful they are and how much these cards helped them. From helping people sleep, to multidimensional travelling and help letting go. They help clear blocked chakras and energy, ground and balance you, awaken your masculine and feminine sides and so much more.

One thing I just love about the cards is that they evolve with you. So it doesn't matter what your energy frequency or vibration is (meaning, where you are in your life or spiritual development / growth), they will continue to work with you and help peel those old layers back, revealing your whole and perfect self. They encourage freedom from your old hurt and pain and help you stay ever grounded in this moment.

Not long after my grandfather passed away I was inspired to paint a painting of the aurora (night lights over the pole regions). I painted it with lots of pink and a beautiful white beam of light in the centre. If you have a pack of my Healing Energy Cards you will know this one to be 28. White Light. Although with my grandfather in mind when painting the original for this card, I never stop being surprised by what this specific card can do to help people. Many people select it who have spinal problems, the beam of white light helps align and purify the energy within the spinal column, deeply healing the area. There is something truly magical about this card.

Another special card is number 7. Self Love. This drawing was inspired by a shamanic journey meditation I had experienced a few years before. During the visual meditation I saw myself sitting on a grassy hill, next to a tree and drawing the beautiful view before me. I then observed the sky turning into a ceiling and a pair of golden energy hands scooped me into this other world. Although I couldn't see any other beings, I sensed their presence as I walked past white dome shaped buildings. I was drawn into a main one, which I call the Temple. Here, in the open space I sat in a chair that was provided. Directly above me was an opening where pure love flowed inside and filled me up with love. Time seemed to stand still and I was in this space for what seemed like months. I was inspired to add this powerful drawing to the Healing Energy Cards to assist with self love and to inspire others to open their hearts while giving and receiving love.

Some of the cards came to me in dreams and visions and others just created themselves on the art paper. For example, one of my favourite cards number 2. Soul Chakras came to me clearly in a vision. I saw a pair of feet, looking at them from the soles, with red chakras in them and tree roots weaving around in the background. I drew what I saw in my mind and again was surprised at how much grounding and balancing energy the drawing contained.

An often confronting card number 17, Time Tunnels came to me on a power day. It was the opening of an energetic gateway on the 17th of October 2006. At the time I connected with some online friends and clients and we did a mass connection, along with many other people around the world at that time. During this massive connection via our intentions I had a vision of this drawing and was told that we as humans can use this card to travel back in time to heal and change the codes of the past. And we will also be able to travel to the future to help create it the way we choose it to be.

There is only one card in the deck that I didn't create, and that is number 14. Male Support. My young son painted this; he was about 8 years old at the time. As soon as I saw it I knew it had to be in the deck. I love this card, it brings with it a male energy and perspective which is something different and unique. This card reminds us of our support networks and can also help clear blocks between the father and son connections.

In 2010 I added another sixteen cards to the pre-existing Healing Energy Cards. These extra cards bought forth new energy about love, relationships, birthing the new and accessing deeper energy levels.

Energy is moving so quickly now. The power of our thoughts and intentions are being created in our lives so quickly and sometimes instantly.

Look out for a book all about Healing Energy Cards in the future.

Chapter 15 - The Modern Shaman

A few years ago one of my Canadian clients described me as a *'modern shaman'* and this term really stuck with me. Right from the moment my spiritual teacher *Red Eagle* came into my dream and wanted to be drawn, I have been very interested in shamanism. In 2002 I began connecting with a beautiful local shamanic drumming group. From my very first visit I was mesmerised by the hoop drum and it wasn't very long before I knew that I had to connect with my own.

I began to connect deeply with my drum. Her name came through to me, as *'heartbeat'* and I painted a wolf on her. Wolf is the protector of my drum and whatever I am doing with her at the time of drumming.

On a personal level I worked with my drum all the time. I would experiment and listen for sound changes in the beat when working over my body or in rooms. At one stage my connection with my drum was so strong, that I felt she was an extension of my own body. I trust the drum immensely and allow *Heartbeat* to guide me as I play. I love working with the space, drumming in various places I am led to around a room. I also like to work with the surface of the drum, listening and feeling for 'sweet spots' that call me to be played. The tempo or speed is also important as I play. I don't like being restricted by things; for example, being told that a shamanic journey has to be a certain amount of beats per second. I have always trusted my intuition and the connection I have with my drum in regards to the tempo and rhythm that is created. I guess this maybe where the 'modern' title comes into play. I take the traditions that I observe and learn from others and then I adapt it to suit my feelings and instincts.

My husband and I regularly drum out in nature, sending healing and love to the Earth. We also regularly use sacred smoke, like a smudge stick or incense to cleanse spaces (rooms) and ourselves. If you, your house or office are feeling flat, stagnant or scattered, why not see if sacred smoke cleansing works for you?

Exercise (viii): Smudging self with sacred smoke

I prefer Myrrh or White sage and all you need to do is hold the intention to cleanse. When you are doing it on yourself, **guide** *(directing the smoke with your hand – not too close to the flame area) the smoke over your body and imagine the smoke cleansing and removing unwanted energies from your aura and energy. Just like you have a shower to cleanse your physical body, the sacred smoke helps cleanse your spiritual or energetic body.*

It is great to do this just prior to meditating, doing a card reading or healing on yourself. This is also helpful if you have just dealt with a person who has made you feel uneasy.

Use the smoke, direct it with your hand, be careful not to burn yourself and trust your intuition.

Exercise (ix): Smudging a room with sacred smoke

So many people talk to me about their home or workplace and how stale the energy feels in a certain room or area. I often remind them that they can use sacred smoke (smudge stick or incense) and even if you don't have smoke around or you just don't like it, then you can use a feather you find outside, a leaf, or your hand. Don't limit yourself just to smoke in this and the above exercise.

This is great to do every now and then in your home, office or when you are moving into a new home.

I usually like to start at the front entrance or at an area that feels right to me. Then using the sacred smoke in my left hand, I sweep the smoke up and down with my right hand, a few feet away from the walls. Over the doors I like to do a protective cross requesting that **'only love and light may enter here.'** *Sometimes I will feel like doing this over windows too, especially if a burglar has broken in there sometime in the past.*

As I work my way around every room, and every corner in the house, I pay special attention to 'stagnant' areas where people or animals don't tend to go much. For example: behind couches or television units. As you do this imagine any impurities and old energies leaving through your intention.

This is a very powerful exercise and is also wonderful to do if you are having present issues with members of your house. Maybe smudging their room when they are at school or work will help bring more peace and harmony into your household.

As a *modern shaman* I feel a sense of duty to send as much love, healing, strength and peace to the planet as she needs it. I often embed crystals into the ground, send healing to the earth and nature and am very aware of my surroundings.

With my shaman tools like my hoop drum, rattle, hawk's wing, working with my power animals and sacred smoke I am creating the cultural me that I want to be. I love taking off my shoes and drumming on the sand or on grass. I feel that these days many people are forgetting about their connection with the earth and nature. To me, this connection is so important. Nature reflects to me anything that I may be personally stuck with in my life, so I find it a beautiful way to self heal. I become very inspired by the trees and colours in nature. I feel that this deep connection I have helps me stay ever present in this moment. By keeping my feet firmly planted on the earth, helps me stay in the here and now.

The more grounded and connected we are with this moment, the deeper we can go in meditation. When we are grounded and meditate, we can access amazing wisdom and even travel to other dimensions and galaxies.

I had an interesting experience in mid 2008. My sister Caroline and I were taking our children – five between us, North to our grandmother's home for lunch. We wouldn't all fit in one car, so Caroline drove in front and I followed. The drive was winding along this beautiful valley in North Eastern Tasmania. We were travelling slowly behind an old vehicle, when we reached one of the only straight stretches of road on the trip, Caroline and I overtook this car. Caroline being in front, proceeded first, and then I followed, it was all clear until I was level with the vehicle being overtaken. I was shocked when another car pulled out into my lane a little further up the road, right in my path. I put my foot down and luckily made it to safety in time. That has been the closest I have ever been to a car accident. Breathing a huge sigh of relief we continued on the road. It was only around a few more corners that we reached a section of road that had something in the middle of it. I slowed down and saw a huge Hawk's wing waving to me. This poor Hawk had been hit by a car, I couldn't believe it. There was nowhere to pull over at the time, so we continued on.

Once we got to our grandmother's house, Caroline and I talked about the road trip, and we mentioned the Hawk, I told her I would look again for it on the way back. After spending a wonderful afternoon with our grandmother, treated to her wonderful cooking and sweets, we returned to the road, returning home. It was several hours after I first saw the Hawk, so you can understand my surprise when we rounded the corner and there was this amazing Hawk's wing waving at me again. I felt like it was waving just for me. It was incredible!

Caroline and I pulled over to the side of the road, and with sadness that the Hawk was in spirit, I felt that I had been guided to this spot at this time. I could feel the presence of Hawk around this area very strongly, and I asked permission to work with one of Hawk's wings and feathers for my work. I was granted permission from Hawk in spirit. I carefully pulled this huge Hawk from the centre of the road and freed one of its wings. Our children collected some stray feathers and I said my thanks to this amazing creature for the gift I had been given. This Hawk was huge. One wing spanned as long as my arm. Just amazing! I work with my sacred Hawk's wing quite a lot when clearing energy and healing. I also sometimes dance with it in celebration of my Power Animals.

A power animal is like a spirit guide however it is in animal form. Most people, if not all, have at least one power animal. Sometimes they are called animal totems too. Hawk shares with me its medicine when needed.

If you see a lot of one particular animal or insect around during a specific time, it may be an external sign that you have that particular animal working with you in Power Animal form (in spirit). You can browse the Internet and search for that particular animal along with the words; 'power animal' or 'animal totem' to learn more about possible reasons why that animal is with you. You may be surprised at what you discover!

My shaman essence is the solid foundation that holds me in place. I am forever grateful for my journey, this path, this beautiful planet and nature.

Chapter 16 - Twin Flames

When I was young and couldn't properly see,
I was poked and prodded for being me.

This left an old scar which was embedded inside,
And often at times I would love to just hide!

But now is the time, for in truth I am ready,
To get back on my feet, yes, nice and steady.

I stand tall as the beauty that I eternally am,
Across the great channel of water I swam.

To reach the side of sun and grace,
Where I can truly reveal my face!

Lee-Anne Peters

It doesn't seem to be any accident that I am writing this chapter on the second year anniversary of my Twin Flame, Cory and my reconnection.

The previous poem I wrote a couple of years ago, and I feel it best describes how I used to feel in life. As a child I lacked confidence although gained a lot more when I studied hairdressing. But one critical thing that was lacking in my life was acceptance. I was married to a man I met in college and we were together for fifteen years. During our time together we had two children and had some fun adventures. However I never ever felt I could truly be myself. For me, there was a constant 'put down' of how I looked, why I wore those clothes, why would I say that and so on. Our relationship was hot and cold, yet during it I learnt a lot about myself, my passions and what I did want from life. Deep down I knew we wouldn't be together forever. Our relationship was more of a brother / sister one from my perspective and it felt okay to be living like that while I worked out what I wanted from my life.

Over the past decade I had occasionally dreamt of another man. A man who I hadn't seen (physically), for a very long time, in fact, for several lifetimes. I had that knowing within my heart, but always knew that it wasn't the right time and that I had to focus on my life passions and purpose for now.

For me this feeling stepped up several notches around 2003 when I was getting signs from all directions about the connection of *'one true love'* energy. At the time I was cleaning holiday cabins in the caravan park my family lived in for two years and the song by *Missy Higgins 'The Special Two'* used to play all the time on the radio when I worked. I remember being in tears and feeling such a strong resonance with this song. Within me, I missed something very deeply. And around the same time, during a meditation, I saw a vision that made me know that another part of 'me' was out there on the other side of the world. I missed this part. Friends told me that it was probably a merging feeling with Self after all the self healing I had been doing regarding separation and things, but it didn't sit right, I knew that I had another part of my soul somewhere.

Even though I was sad at the thought of only having half of myself, I continued on with my life. I continued to self heal and explore feelings and memories that surfaced. I also became more creative and trusting in my intuition.

It wasn't before another five years past that things would drastically change and the other half of myself and I would reunite.

I was growing extremely restless in my marriage and for the final three months of it I was being put down more and struggling to even try and be happy. And for the three months I continued to ask my spiritual guides to help me get out! I didn't want to hurt my ex husband or my children, so I needed the transition to be as smooth as possible. Spirit continued to tell me that it was *'not long now and that soon the man I had been waiting for would come into my life.'* I asked how I would know who this person was. They said that; *he was a client, from overseas and I would just know!* These messages would be repeated to me constantly.

It turned out that exactly three months prior to the date of 'reconnection' with my Twin Flame, a young man from Texas in the United States found my website in the strangest way and booked a healing session with me via distance. The healing session was like any other I have done, looking back on it there were a lot of synchronicities and signs in it for us both. The three months brought a nice friendship as he joined my online community and attended online meditations, which I facilitated regularly at the time.

Three months to the date after the first healing session was booked, Cory sent me an email to ask my advice about a meditation vision he had experienced recently. We met online and talked about it through instant texting on my online community. I explored this vision with him and saw that it was all about a past life that we had together in Atlantis many thousands of years ago. This 'remembering' bought forth many emotions for us, and it was lovely to remember.

I knew within me that something special had happened, however it wasn't until the next day when my heart was so full of love that I realised that he was the one I had been waiting for. I had never felt so much *love* in my life. Meanwhile, only a few days earlier I woke up one morning and told my ex-husband that it was over. It was quite painful to see him crying and begging, and his affirmations that he would change, but these words fell on deaf ears, I had heard them many times before, yet no changes were made. I came across cold to him, but I had to be. I had to detach myself from the drama and stick to my truth. I knew that if I followed my heart and truth that everything would work out. It would be up to him as to how long it took, but for me and my children I knew we were all stepping into a brighter and happier life. It took some months for my ex to realise this. I wanted to make it as easy for us all as possible, and this energy that I put out there in my thoughts, words and actions really helped things become much smoother than they could have been.

What surprised me the most was how much the end of our marriage affected family and friends. It was quite interesting to observe their reactions and even their total rejection of me. But all the while I continued to breathe and walk my truth.

As one door closes another opens. And this was very much the case for me here. Having courageously ended a long term relationship and within a week opening my heart to such love with my Twin Flame was incredible.

It was ten weeks before Cory came to live with me in Australia. The timing was perfect as I had just moved into a new house and things were slowly settling with the separation of my ex.

I flew to Sydney and met Cory there on his flight from Houston. We dreamed of this meeting over the ten weeks prior to our physical connection and it was perfect. We were together again!

We learnt that as twin flames come together that they have an important task of helping other flames come together too. They will do this in many unique ways, and for us it is about us sharing our story and being ourselves. During our time together we have done a lot of meditating and learnt a lot about twin flames.

Twin flames connect on every level possible. There is no level that clashes. So the physical, emotional, mental and spiritual levels are connected. If you connect with someone, maybe who you 'think' is your flame on three of those levels, but let's say that your 'flame' doesn't have similar spiritual values as you, then you may not be twin flames. In some cases you may have 'pre-chosen' before you both came into this lifetime not to physically unite this time. Maybe you had other things to attend to personally. The truth of this can be difficult for many to grasp, especially if they think they know who their Twin Flame is. The problem is the 'thinking' bit. If you can step away from what the lower or ego mind thinks and into what your heart feels and knows then you may get a clearer idea of what is happening.

For both Cory and I, we resonate perfectly on every level, and that resonation continues to grow as we get to know each other physically. You see the twin flame is always connected on a soul level, and it's your souls who do everything they can to bring the two of you back together on the physical level. You can communicate and connect with your twin flame on a spiritual level during your dream state or in meditation, prior to physical reunion.

One thing (among many others) that is very sacred to me about my twin flame relationship is that we accept each other totally for who we are. There is an inner knowing and acceptance that we love all of who we are as individuals. We never say 'I love you more" because in our hearts and knowing, we know that we love each other the same. Imagine being with someone who loves you totally for being you. They don't tell you that you shouldn't have done this or that, they just be there and allow you to be you. It is perfect, and the way these sacred twin flame relationships are.

You may think that this is a fairytale romance and that this love cannot exist in your life, you have been hurt too many times and this is the way it will be for you forever. If that is what you believe, then that is what you create. I ask you to challenge and question any 'beliefs' that you hold regarding sacred love and open your heart to heal and feel.

I am going to take you through some heart healing now. If you know that you have another part of yourself 'out there', if you have been hurt or wounded in love in the past or if you would like to learn to love yourself more, this may help you. If your heart isn't feeling bruised or wounded, then please either absorb what you need from this exercise or skip forward.

Exercise (x): Healing your heart

Breathe a deep and relaxing breath. Feel the air enter through your nose or mouth and feel it exit too as you breathe out. Become aware of your breathing.

Allow your vision to soften on these words and feel your body become nice and heavy and relaxed.

When you breathe in now bring your focus directly to your heart chakra. You may remember that this is your centre for love of self, others and all creation. Become sensitive to this area, both the front and the back of your heart chakra. Notice if there is any tightness, tension or emotions stored in there. Don't judge what you see or feel, just allow these energies to come to the surface.

*Hold your hands out in front of you as we ask your hands to **fill with healing light**, and when you are ready either physically or using your imagination place one (or both) of your hands onto your heart. Sit here for a few moments, breathing and feeling. Take your time.*

When you feel ready; imagine, see or feel a coloured light enter your heart via your physical or etheric hand/s. Allow any colour to come forward that feels right for you in this moment. Try not to think what the colour should be, but allow it to be the colour that you need right now. If you do this exercise again a different colour will most likely present itself. Trust the colour to come to you.

Allow this colour to deeply penetrate your heart chakra. Here it heals all old love wounds and scars, lifting any old issues and blocks that are affecting the love you have towards yourself or others. Feel and know the light is washing them away, helping you let go and helping you be free.

Take as much time as you need. As the intenseness of the old energy subsides, feel the energy shift a little. Where the old energy was, there is beautiful and new refreshing energy (from your hand) replacing the wounds and sadness with love and acceptance.

Let the light flow into place and boost the light and love in every cell within your heart: both physically and energetically. Breathe this love around your heart, feel it begin to spin as a vortex of light. Feel your heart open to giving and receiving love.

Cry those tears of joy and celebrate the beautiful essence of light that you are.

Expand this feeling of love around into the rest of your body using the power of your breathing.

Stay in this space for as long as you need to, by holding here. Don't read on until you are ready to settle back into your everyday life.

When you are ready, thank the energies for their help, gently remove your hand and continue to feel the love in your heart and body.

Take this feeling into every step you take. Implement these changes you feel into your everyday life.

Please return to this exercise anytime you feel you would like to do more healing on your heart.

With an open heart feel your connection with the other half of your soul. Breathe and feel a connection, you may have trouble describing what you feel, and this is okay. Whether the other half of your soul is sitting right beside you or is on the other side of the world, space does not matter. You are always connected.

The soul is pure, perfect and complete. For Cory and I, our soul split into two aspects a long, long time ago. Long before we entered into the Earth for our first lifetime here, this was around 11,000 years ago. We spent several lives during that time experiencing lessons and learning on this earth plane. After we complete our mission, which will be at the end of this lifetime, we will merge as 'One' again and return to our home in the stars.

Many twin flames and sacred loves are uniting at this time. *Why now and not as much in the past several thousand years?* Well, during very ancient civilisations the energy here was lighter, the frequency of the planet and all inhabitants began to get denser and denser. I was shown in a vision once that even if the Ancient city of Atlantis was still functioning at this time, we would not see it in this dense energy space.

The great news is that the energy frequency is lightening and at a very rapid rate. We are evolving into something beyond words. These are exciting times to be living. Not only are more and more twin flames reuniting and helping us anchor divine love on this planet, but we are moving out of the lies and corruption that plagued this planet for far too long and are moving into truth, love and acceptance. We are moving out of the denseness quite rapidly.

I feel the changes must start with us as individuals. I don't worry about what is happening here or there around the world. I do my best to stay neutral but informed about the truth. If I worry, fear or stress about the wars or disasters, then I am sending that lower vibrating energy to that situation or the people involved. This is something I do not want to do. So I send love, peace and harmony and choose not to be caught in the drama.

It is important that we break the cycles. Whether these are: negative thoughts, words or actions, that we may have been caught in. Acknowledge you do this, and then make changes necessary. When we as individuals make changes to ourselves and the way we react or respond, then this helps change the planetary grid. We are individual stars that make up the whole. As individual stars we have more power to change than many may think. It has been too many years of corruption and controlling agendas that have made us believe that we can't do anything. That we need to look outside of ourselves for someone to worship, to make decisions for us and so forth. WE have the power to change the world. BE that change you want to see. You will inspire and empower others to be themselves and to be that change too. This then reaches out to more and more people.

We don't need to force our ideas onto others, simply be yourself and others will join you if they resonate with your energy, teachings or words. Everyone has a choice and that choice must be honoured and respected.

Twin flames are unique and are not for the few but for the many. Twin flames are uniting on mass. Twin flames contain little to no old residual hurt and pain (what we used to call karma), they come together free of this. When you look into your twin flame's eyes it is like looking into a mirror. Often physical markings are reflected from one flame to another. There will be things you both like or dislike that will harmonise with the other. There will be characteristics that nourish what you always felt would be your ultimate mate or partner in life.

Sharing my life with my beautiful twin flame for two years now feels like eons. Time becomes stretched and altered in this space of love. Our love and connection continues to deepen every moment. The simple things like a touch, word or action means the world to twin flames.

We had a beautiful vision when we first reconnected. We saw both of us tending to our own 'campfire.' We experienced what we needed to and learnt as we journeyed on during this lifetime and others as individuals. We placed logs on our own fires, and learnt how to keep them alight when things got tough and the rain almost put our fires out. When reconnecting together we expanded our campfires until they became one large fire that we both tended together. We nourished each other's fire, which represented our life experience, journey and our physical, emotional, mental and spiritual needs. Each day our fire expands, grows and glows brighter than ever before. I could never imagine feeling more love than I did that very first moment of reconnecting, but it does continue to grow and grow every moment.

Chapter 17 - Visions for the future

As we head into the powerful 2011 I have many visions for the future and what various roles Temple of Balance 'plays' in this. Because I have the ability to see into the future, I have seen many visions of big things we will be doing, yet right now I am in the process of building up to them. At times it can be a little frustrating trying to work out a way to get from point A to point Z, especially when you have visions of point Z so clearly. However I learn to step back from that future point in time and be all I can be in the here and now. I make sure I take small steps each day and as I do this I know I am stepping into points B, C and D, knowing that these will lead me ultimately to point Z. I am also very flexible so even though I may be aiming for point Z, when I reach point M and if something slightly different opens up, I take it. I feel that being determined and focused is important, but being flexible is just as important. Sometimes our paths change from the original plan and there is nothing wrong with this.

The immediate vision for Temple of Balance is to get products into your hands, like this book, oracle cards, tarot cards and maybe another book or two. I see this evolving into Temple of Balance Publishing, as you may notice on the back of this book. You see, in the past twelve months my husband Cory and I have travelled interstate to teach and help inspire others through workshops and events. These have been amazing and I just love seeing the transformation in people from when they walk in at the beginning and when they walk out. It is inspiring to me. In that time I have seen many people blossom and grow while they follow their own dreams and passions. As a teacher this is very rewarding.

During our last teaching visit to Sydney a couple of months ago, I held a shamanic healing day. During this day I facilitated a meditation to help the participants connect with their power animals. In this meditation I could feel an animal sitting on my head. I asked what this animal was, and then this little pink face popped down and looked into mine. It was a possum. He told me that after this teaching tour it would be time for me to stay at home and finish this book and do a couple of other projects. He said that I mustn't teach out of state again until this book is finished. Possum was sitting on my head to make sure I stayed put! If I had thoughts of organising an event interstate prior to the time when my book would be released, he would fluff his tail up my nose and tickle me there! So I have committed to possum's help and remained focused on this project. Between you and I – the possum tail fluffing up my nose got quite irritating at times!

I have so many visions and plans that it can be hard to know where to flow next.

In the long term I see Temple of Balance doing tours overseas in Europe, America and Canada. This is still some way off, however I know it will happen in the coming years.

For Temple of Balance here in our home state of Tasmania, which is a beautiful heart shaped island off the South of Australia, Cory and I look forward to the moment when we can become self sufficient in our own home. It is important to me that we live more in harmony with Earth. I am not interested in concrete and structures that look and feel so unnatural. I have a deep yearning to live in harmony with this beautiful planet and with the nature surrounding wherever we will be living. On this rural setting I see us building our Temple of Balance as a healing retreat.

I feel we are living in exciting times, although challenging at times, within every challenge is an opportunity to grow, learn and be more of who you are.

I focus on writing this book, drawing & designing 78 tarot cards, drawing and designing oracle cards, organising Reflect Radio, meditation groups, guest speaker / radio interviews, looking after my two children, honouring my marriage and connection with myself, managing twelve facebook groups, working with clients, website designing and maintaining, managing events and various other projects. Lately I hear so many people complaining that they have too much on. With time management and making sure everything you are doing fits in with your integrity in that moment, it won't feel like a burden. Everything will fit and flow into place. With all I have going on I only feel slightly overwhelmed every now and then and I take the afternoon / day off or spend some time in nature.

When we listen to our body, make sure we do a bit of something towards our projects / dreams most days, they do start to complete. New opportunities do present themselves and you are living fully in your passion and following your dreams.

Success, in whatever definition you feel success is, rarely happens to someone who complains about what they are doing, or who doesn't do anything. Success comes from commitment, taking action and listening to your body so you can keep in balance.

I believe that we really can do anything, and that we are the Master Creators of our life.

Take steps today to make your dreams come true!

Biography

Lee-Anne Peters

Visionary artist, radio host, author, teacher and healer, Lee-Anne Peters (nee Willson) was born and still lives on the heart shaped island of Tasmania, off the South Coast of Australia. She shares her life with her beautiful husband (Cory), son (Sean) and daughter (Madison).

Lee-Anne is the founder of **Temple of Balance**; specialising in letting go, creative therapies, self healing and inspiring your inner strength and freedom. And the founder of **Temple of Balance Radio**!

In 2008 Lee-Anne self published her healing artwork into a set of **Healing Energy Cards**, which are tools for self healing, self transformation and self empowerment. They have helped people from all over the world. In 2010, 16 new cards boosted the original 32 up to 48.

This book, **Temple of Balance the book** is Lee-Anne's first title to be published under Temple of Balance Publishing.

A born entrepreneur Lee-Anne has always been an 'action girl.' Lee-Anne describes this as 'acting on her intuitive impulses.' Her spiritual guides and teachers love this about her. They seed her with ideas and inspirations and she quickly takes action. At the age of 19, Lee-Anne started her short hairdressing career, which only lasted a few years.

It was Lee-Anne's passion as a mother, that gave her time to spend with her children, which then led to other doorways of opportunity opening before her. She spent some time travelling with her young family, including two years living from a caravan while she worked cleaning holiday cabins and doing psychic readings. During this time her spiritual side grew deeper, as she made everlasting connections and began to see the world from a different perspective.

Lee-Anne's ability to draw is a natural talent and the only formal training she had was during art class in high school. Lee-Anne learns a lot from observing others, which helped her adapt to new ways and techniques that suit her method of working. Having drawn spiritual guides for people for the past decade, Lee-Anne feels excited when she hears of people 'stumbling' across her work hanging in a friend's house that they visit.

These days Lee-Anne loves working on a variety of projects with others along with her personal projects. She loves to spend time in nature, drumming and sending love to the Earth. Spending time with her children brings Lee-Anne great joy, as she shares her gifts of art, creating and living a simple life, without the need for the shiniest possessions.

The happiest she has been, is since her Twin Flame came to live with her two years ago. Lee-Anne finds it so comforting and beautiful to share her life with someone who understands and accepts who she is. Cory walks by Lee-Anne's side, honouring every step and choice she makes. Their love continues to blossom and grow.

During this journey Lee-Anne has learnt to completely trust her inner guidance, passions, creativity and the moment. All whilst maintaining balance in her body, mind, emotions and spirit. Lee-Anne looks forward to Temple of Balance growing and expanding in amazing ways. **Temple of Balance the book** is another step on this empowering and inspiring path!

Message from the Author:

Thank you so much for reading and connecting with my very first book! I am incredibly excited about this milestone, and just as I complete this, my next book is being inspired to begin – thanks Universe! This is a wonderful journey and I feel honoured to be sharing it with you.

I trust that you have received what you needed from my story and the exercises shared with you during this writing.

Please browse this book's website for purchasing information, more practical tools, tips, and a place to leave your feedback! http://thebook.templeofbalance.com

I look forward to bring more informative books, cards and products to you, to help you get the most out of your journey, your life experience!

Until next time,

Keep smiling and live from your heart!

Lee-Anne

March 2011

Soul Activation Series

Unlock your Soul's Purpose, Power and Potential!

7 events ~ over 7 days.

Activate your chakras, get back in touch with your core, unlock your creative abilities, spend time with like-minded people and understand more about your life's purpose.

Receive practical and easy-to-use tools to help you in your everyday life. You will activate energy and experience new sensations deeper and higher than anything you have ever experienced.

All this occurs in a very safe space, orchestrated by your host, Temple of Balance (Lee-Anne & Cory).

You will not want to miss this series!

View our upcoming events at www.templeofbalance.com

'A beautiful weekend, great meditations. Well explained. I loved the freedom to talk and contribute, going with the flow. A great way to open up to this part of myself. Thanks again.' Cassie, NSW, Australia

If we aren't coming to country near you soon, please request an event in your area via our website contact form. www.templeofbalance.com

Healing Energy Cards

Empowering tools to help you heal deeply on all levels.

48 hand drawn cards, with a 4 page booklet.

Available to purchase NOW via our website!

http://healingenergycards.templeofbalance.com

28. White Light

Crown & Third Eye Chakras. Spinal Healing with White Light. Love. Support. Indigo. Intuition. Look within. Inner Wisdom. Vision. Trust. Faith. Activation of Kundalini. Memories of loved Ones.
www.templeofbalance.com

Temple of Balance

Specialising in Letting go, Creative Therapies, Self Healing and Inspiring Your Inner Strength and Freedom.

Spirit Guide Drawings

Twin Flame Clearings / Healings

Intuitive Energy Healing

Distant, local or phone sessions

Workshops / Courses / Healing Retreats

Healing Energy Cards

Meditation CD

Crystals

Words of Wisdom

Temple of Balance Radio

Learn more about Temple of Balance at
www.templeofbalance.com

Temple of Balance ~ Inspiring Your Freedom!

Temple of Balance Publishing

Inspiring ~ Creating ~ Empowering

EST 2011

http://publishing.templeofbalance.com